IRAQ AND VIETNAM:
DIFFERENCES, SIMILARITIES, AND INSIGHTS

Jeffrey Record
W. Andrew Terrill

University Press of the Pacific
Honolulu, Hawaii

Iraq and Vietnam:
Differences, Similarities, and Insights

by
Jeffrey Record
W. Andrew Terrill

ISBN: 1-4102-1744-2

Reprinted from the 2004 edition

University Press of the Pacific
Honolulu, Hawaii
http://www.universitypressofthepacific.com

FOREWORD

U.S. political and military difficulties in Iraq have prompted comparisons to the American war in Vietnam. How, in fact, do the two wars compare? What are the differences and similarities, and what insights can be gained from examining them? Does the Vietnam War have instructive lessons for those dealing with today's challenges in Iraq, or is that war simply irrelevant?

In the pages that follow, two highly qualified analysts address these questions. Dr. Jeffrey Record, formerly a civilian pacification advisor in Vietnam and author of books on both the Vietnam and Iraq wars, and W. Andrew Terrill, author and co-author of several SSI studies on Iraq, conclude that the military dimensions of the two conflicts bear little comparison. Among other things, the sheer scale of the Vietnam War in terms of forces committed and losses incurred dwarfs that of the Iraq War. They also conclude, however, that failed U.S. state-building in Vietnam and the impact of declining domestic political support for U.S. war aims in Vietnam are issues pertinent to current U.S. policy in Iraq.

The Strategic Studies Institute is pleased to offer this monograph as a contribution to the national security debate over Iraq.

DOUGLAS C. LOVELACE, JR.
Director
Strategic Studies Institute

BIOGRAPHICAL SKETCH OF THE AUTHOR

JEFFREY RECORD joined the Strategic Studies Institute in August 2003 as Visiting Research Professor. He is a professor in the Department of Strategy and International Security at the U.S. Air Force's Air War College in Montgomery, Alabama. He is the author of six books and a dozen monographs, including: *Making War, Thinking History: Munich, Vietnam, and Presidential Uses of Force from Korea to Kosovo; Revising US Military Strategy: Tailoring Means to Ends; Beyond Military Reform; Hollow Victory, A Contrary View of the Gulf War; The Gulf War; The Gulf War The Wrong War, Why We Lost in Vietnam;* and *Failed States and Casualty Phobia, Implications for U.S. Force Structure and Technology Choices.* Dr. Record has served as Assistant Province Advisor in the Mekong Delta during the Vietnam War, Rockefeller Younger Scholar on the Brookings Institution's Defense Analysis Staff, and Senior Fellow at the Institute for Foreign Policy Analysis, the Hudson Institute, and the BDM International Corporation. He also has extensive Capitol Hill experience, serving as Legislative Assistant for National Security Affairs to Senators Sam Nunn and Lloyd Bentsen, and later as a Professional Staff Member of the Senate Armed Services Committee. Dr. Record received his Doctorate at the Johns Hopkins School of Advanced International Studies.

W. ANDREW TERRILL joined the Strategic Studies Institute in October 2001, and is SSI s Middle East specialist. Prior to his appointment, he served as a senior international security analyst for the International Assessments Division of the Lawrence Livermore National Laboratory (LLNL). In 1998-99, Dr. Terrill also served as a Visiting Professor at the U.S. Air War College on assignment from LLNL. He is a former faculty member at Old Dominion University in Norfolk, Virginia, and has taught adjunct at a variety of other colleges and universities. He is a U.S. Army Reserve lieutenant colonel and a Foreign Area Officer (Middle East). Dr. Terrill has published in numerous academic journals on topics including nuclear proliferation, the Iran-Iraq War, Operation DESERT STORM, Middle Eastern chemical weapons, and ballistic missile proliferation, terrorism, and commando operations. Since 1994, at U.S. State Department invitation, Dr. Terrill has participated in the Middle Eastern Regional Security Track 2 talks, which are part of the Middle East Peace Process. He holds a B.A. from California State Polytechnic University and an M.A. from the University of California, Riverside, both in Political Science. Dr Terrill also holds a Ph.D. in International Relations from Claremont Graduate University, Claremont, California.

SUMMARY

Unfolding events in Iraq have prompted some observers to make analogies to the American experience in the Vietnam War. The United States has, they argue, stumbled into another overseas "quagmire" from which there is no easy or cheap exit.

Reasoning by historical analogy is an inherently risky business because no two historical events are completely alike and because policymakers' knowledge and use of history are often distorted by ignorance and political bias. In the case of Iraq and Vietnam, extreme caution should be exercised in comparing two wars so far apart in time, locus, and historical circumstances. In fact, a careful examination of the evidence reveals that the differences between the two conflicts greatly outnumber the similarities. This is especially true in the strategic and military dimensions of the two wars. There is simply no comparison between the strategic environment, the scale of military operations, the scale of losses incurred, the quality of enemy resistance, the role of enemy allies, and the duration of combat.

Such an emphatic judgment, however, may not apply to at least two aspects of the political dimensions of the Iraq and Vietnam wars: attempts at state-building in an alien culture, and sustaining domestic political support in a protracted war against an irregular enemy. It is, of course, far too early predict whether the United States will accomplish its policy objectives in Iraq and whether public support will "stay the course" on Iraq. But policymakers should be mindful of the reasons for U.S. failure to create a politically legitimate and militarily viable state in South Vietnam, as well as for the Johnson and Nixon administrations' failure to sustain sufficient domestic political support for the accomplishment of U.S. political objectives in Indochina. Repetition of those failures in Iraq could have disastrous consequences for U.S. foreign policy.

IRAQ AND VIETNAM:
DIFFERENCES, SIMILARITIES, AND INSIGHTS

Jeffrey Record and W. Andrew Terrill

INTRODUCTION

Many of those who questioned the U.S. invasion of Iraq and now doubt the chances of creating a stable and prosperous democracy in that country have invoked America's experience in Vietnam as an analogy. In their view, the United States has yet again stumbled into a foreign quagmire--a protracted and indecisive political and military struggle from which the United States is unlikely to extricate itself absent expenditure of considerable blood and treasure and abandonment of its policy objectives.

Conversely, proponents of the Iraq War and optimists over Iraq's future have dismissed the Vietnam analogy as misleading, even irrelevant. For them, the differences between the two wars vastly outnumber the similarities; the appropriate analogy is not Vietnam, but rather the total destruction of Nazi Germany and Imperial Japan and their transformation into democratic allies. Still others believe some elements of Vietnam are present in Iraq--e.g., both wars involved counterinsurgency operations, but not others--e.g., there is no counterpart in the Iraq War to North Vietnam, and that the non-analogous elements dominate.[1]

The Vietnam War's entry into the debate over the Iraq War and its aftermath probably was inevitable. The Vietnam War continues to influence American attitudes toward the use of force overseas, and the analogy of Vietnam has been a staple of critics of U.S. intervention in foreign internal wars since the fall of Saigon in 1975. The Vietnam War was moreover a defining foreign policy event for the generation of political and military leaders now in power. It was also the last major counterinsurgency experience of the U.S. Army and Marine Corps, which re-encountered the counterinsurgency mission in Iraq.

Are there instructive comparisons between the U.S. military and political experiences in Vietnam in the 1960s and the challenges it faces in Iraq today? If so, can those comparisons usefully inform

1

current U.S. policy in Iraq? Are there lessons from America's defeat in Vietnam that can be applied to promote U.S. success in Iraq? Indeed, what *were* the lessons of the Vietnam War?

At first glance the contrasts between the Vietnam and Iraq wars would seem to overwhelm the similarities. To begin with, Vietnam in the 1960s was a country with a long national history and powerful national identity forged by centuries of fierce resistance to foreign rule and domination. The Communists had successfully mobilized that nationalism against the French (as they were subsequently to do against the United States) and had developed a doctrine of protracted irregular warfare that pitted Vietnamese strengths against Western weaknesses. In contrast, Iraq is a relatively young state plagued by ethnic and religious divisions that threaten national unity.

In Vietnam the United States went to war with a pre-Goldwater-Nichols conscript military against a highly experienced, skilled, disciplined, and operationally flexible enemy that enjoyed enormous external material support and considerable international legitimacy. In Iraq, highly-professional U.S. joint forces quickly overwhelmed a politically isolated and militarily incompetent foe. Additionally, whereas in Vietnam the nature of war evolved from an insurgency into a predominantly conventional conflict, in Iraq it moved exactly--and quickly--in the opposite direction, from major conventional combat into an insurgent war.

The nature of insurgent warfare in Vietnam and Iraq also differed. In Vietnam, the Communists waged a classic, peasant-based, centrally directed, three-stage, Maoist model insurgency, culminating in a conventional military victory. The Communists also had a clear and well-publicized political, economic, and social agenda. In Iraq, small, scattered, and disparate groups wage a much smaller-scale war of ambushes, assassinations, car bombings, and sabotage against U.S. and other coalition forces and reconstruction targets, including Iraqis collaborating with coalition forces. Nor do the insurgents have an explicit set of war aims.

U.S. war aims and freedom of military action were also much more limited in Vietnam than they are in Iraq. The United States sought only to defend South Vietnam, not overthrow North Vietnam. American military power in Indochina moreover was checked by the threat of Chinese intervention, and more broadly by the Soviet threat worldwide. Today, the United States enjoys uncontested global military primacy and seeks nothing less than revolutionary regime change in Iraq.

In Vietnam, the United States committed a peak-strength force of over 500,000 troops and withdrew after 8 years of major combat operations that incurred 58,000 American dead and 305,000 wounded.[2] In Iraq, U.S. forces overwhelmed Iraqi military resistance in 3 weeks and continue to conduct operations against a small and manageable insurgency, all at a cost of — as of mid-April 2004 — 685 dead.

From neither a strategic nor an operational standpoint does there appear to be any significant and meaningful comparison between Iraq and Vietnam. The wars and the backdrop of the global distribution of power against which they were waged were as different as night and day.

It is from the political standpoint that Vietnam may harbor some pertinent lessons, or at least warnings, for U.S. policymakers on Iraq. This seems especially the case in the areas of legitimacy and sustainability. The United States is now seeking to do in Iraq what it failed to do in South Vietnam: create and sustain an indigenous government and political order that the Iraqi people will accept as legitimate and successfully fight to defend. The Republic of Vietnam was a Cold War creation of the United States and for its brief and corrupt 20-year history remained utterly dependent for its survival on America military power and economic and technical assistance. As such, it was a politically attractive target to the Communists, who claimed that the regime in Saigon was illegitimate. In the end, there were simply not enough South Vietnamese who were prepared to fight, and if necessary die, to preserve the non-Communist political order as it was then configured.

It did not help, of course, that the United States eventually abandoned South Vietnam to its fate, which brings us to the issue of sustainability. The Communist strategy of protracted war succeeded in part because it correctly identified the American center of gravity as public opinion. The limited and abstract nature of U.S. objectives in Indochina meant that there were limits to the domestic political sustainability of the American war effort. Over time, the combination of continuing losses of blood and treasure with no apparent definitive policy progress turned public and congressional opinion against the war, at least as it was being conducted. This situation prompted a steady withdrawal of U.S. forces and accession to a negotiated settlement that effectively abandoned South Vietnam to its Communist foe. (The Paris Peace Accord of January 1973 mandated the withdrawal of all U.S. combat forces from South Vietnam, while leaving in place there over 200,000 North Vietnamese Army troops. Under the circumstances, it was unrealistic to expect South Vietnamese forces alone to accomplish what U.S. and South Vietnamese forces had failed to accomplish after 8 years of major combat operations.)

State-building in Iraq is still a work in progress, and it is impossible at this juncture to make conclusive judgments on the domestic political sustainability of U.S. policy in Iraq. Though the United States incurred unexpected casualties and occupation costs in post-Saddam Iraq, they bear no comparison with those of the Vietnam War. On the other hand, by virtue of the Vietnam War (and subsequent failed interventions in Lebanon and Somalia), U.S. public and congressional tolerance levels for protracted, indecisive conflict are not what they were in 1965.

This monograph seeks to identify and examine key comparisons between the challenges the United States faces in Iraq today and those it confronted in Vietnam for the purpose of offering historical insights to U.S. policymakers responsible for policy and operations in Iraq. We believe that differences between Iraq and Vietnam can be just as important as similarities in providing policy insights.

The monograph assesses differences and similarities in the following areas: relative U.S. military power; war aims; nature, duration, and scale of the war; U.S. manpower loss rates; the enemy; military operations; pacification; role of indigenous and international allies; challenges of state-building; and challenges of sustaining domestic political support. It ends with conclusions and recommendations.

COMPARISONS: THEN AND NOW

Relative U.S. Military Power.

Profound differences separate the global and regional military balances of the Vietnam and Iraq wars. The balances of 1965 significantly limited U.S. freedom of military action; those of 2003, in contrast, encouraged preventive war. In 2003 the United States enjoyed uncontested conventional military supremacy, global in scope. As the sole remaining superpower and possessor of the most combat-effective conventional military forces on the planet, the United States was not militarily dependent, as it had been during the Cold War, on major allied force contributions. Furthermore, it could use force with strategic and operational impunity relative to the constraints America faced in Vietnam in 1965, which was a Cold War-driven intervention.

During the Cold War, U.S. freedom of military action was checked in much of Eurasia by the Soviet Union and China, the dominant land powers in their respective regions. Any local war with a lesser Communist state risked provoking escalation by Moscow or Beijing. Additionally, war with the Soviet Union risked uncontrollable escalation into a mutually suicidal nuclear exchange. In the case of the Vietnam War, fear of provoking direct Chinese and even Soviet intervention significantly restrained the application of U.S. military power. President Lyndon Johnson, mindful of China's surprise intervention in the Korean War and its disastrous political consequences for the Truman administration, prudently restricted the pace and parameters of the U.S. air war against North Vietnam for fear of igniting China's entry into the war.[3] Even absent direct Chinese or Soviet military intervention, Beijing and Moscow provided massive assistance that enabled the Vietnamese Communists to sustain military operations, modernize their forces, and "attrit" American will.

In contrast, Saddam Hussein's Iraq was isolated in 2003; his former superpower patron had disappeared and his military forces, largely wrecked in 1991, had been subsequently denied access to modernizing technologies. Moreover, the post-1991 U.S. threats to support a military coup in Iraq appear to have prevented Saddam from training his units in urban warfare, which he seemed to view as regime-threatening.[4] Training in general was not a priority for the Iraqi military, and this shortcoming quickly became apparent after the beginning of the U.S. invasion of 2003. Thus in 2003 U.S. and coalition forces required less than a month to crush Iraqi conventional military resistance, take Baghdad, and overthrow Saddam Hussein.

At the regional level, the military balance between the United

States and the Vietnamese Communists was not nearly so favorable in the 1960s. Most U.S. "general purpose" forces were tied down across a host of Cold War commitments outside of Southeast Asia; indeed, at the peak of U.S. force deployments in 1969, the U.S. Army withheld only one division in strategic reserve in the United States. The Communists benefited from massive Soviet, Chinese, and other Bloc materiel and manpower assistance, including transfers of highly competitive Soviet military technologies, and they had also perfected a style of warfare that capitalized on both their own strengths as well as U.S. weaknesses. Additionally, though there was never any question that the United States had the power to destroy North Vietnam, the limited scope of U.S. war aims (in contrast to the total war the Communists waged) and fear of escalation encouraged imposition of considerable restraints on the U.S. application of force. Moreover, by the early 1970s the war and U.S. and South Vietnamese military and pacification initiatives had crippled (though not destroyed) the original insurgency in the South.

War Aims.

A major contrast between the Vietnam and Iraq wars is the political objectives sought. In the 1960s, the United States was the counter-revolutionary power in Southeast Asia; it sought to preserve the non-communist status quo in South Vietnam by containing the expansion of Communism south of the 17th Parallel that separated the Communist North from South Vietnam. In 2003, the United States was the revolutionary power in the Middle East by virtue of its proclaimed intention to democratize Iraq for the purpose of providing an inspirational model for the rest of the Arab world. In contrast to U.S. war aims in not only Vietnam but also in the 1991 Gulf War, containment was rejected in favor of radical regime change. Democracy was not an issue in the Vietnam War. Rather, the United States was prepared to tolerate an absence of democracy in South Vietnam (and in many of its other Third World client states) so long as it promoted policies favorable to U.S. objectives in the Cold War.

The aim of regime *preservation* in the Vietnam War, which boiled down to the related but quite different challenges of pacifying an indigenous insurgency and coercing North Vietnam to cease its military intervention in South Vietnam, required a massive and protracted military effort against a determined and skilled foe. In contrast, the more ambitious objective of regime change in Iraq entailed a much smaller and shorter war to defeat Iraq's conventional military forces, although the abrupt and complete collapse of Saddam Hussein's regime created a vacuum of political power which afforded regime remnants and other anti-occupation groups the opportunity to mount insurgent attacks on U.S. forces and reconstruction targets.

There were other differences in war aims. The primary declared objective of Operation IRAQI FREEDOM was to disarm Iraq of its suspected weapons of mass destruction (WMD). Such weapons were not an issue in the Vietnam War, which was a struggle over territory. Additionally, the war on Iraq was justified as part of a larger war on terrorism that was sparked by the horrendous al-Qaeda attacks on the United States of September 11, 2001. Homeland security from external terrorist attack was not an issue in the 1960s, though Vietnamese Communist forces did conduct terrorist attacks against Americans and South Vietnamese government targets in Vietnam, including South Vietnam government officials and U.S. civilian personnel. Such attacks, however, were peripheral to main force Viet Cong and North Vietnamese military operations in the South.

Perhaps the most publicly repeated U.S. war aim in Vietnam was that of maintaining the credibility of U.S. defense commitments worldwide. As stated apocalyptically by Secretary of State Dean Rusk,

> There can be no serious debate about the fact that we have a commitment to assist the South Vietnamese to resist aggression from the North. . . . The integrity of the U.S. commitment is the principal pillar of peace throughout the world. If that commitment becomes unreliable, the communist world would draw conclusions that would lead to our ruin and almost certainly to a catastrophic war.[5]

The defense of South Vietnam, argued the Johnson administration, demonstrated the willingness of the United States to go to war on behalf of prior declared commitments to do so; failure to defend South Vietnam would cause other American allies to question the credibility of the U.S. commitment to their defense. It would also encourage communist advances elsewhere in the Third World; indeed, abandoning South Vietnam would, it was argued, have a "domino" effect in the rest of Southeast Asia, with the Communists toppling one government after the other in the region.

The credibility of U.S. defense commitments worldwide was not an issue in 2003. The Communist threat that gave rise to U.S. Cold War alliance system had all but disappeared, and Operation IRAQI FREEDOM was not a response to Iraqi aggression. On the contrary, it was a preventive war designed to forestall what was believed to be Iraq's eventual acquisition of nuclear weapons and the expansion of a perceived Iraqi biological weapons capability. That said, the war did serve the purpose of demonstrating U.S. willingness to use force on behalf of a newly proclaimed security doctrine that embraced the principle of anticipatory military action against nuclear weapons-aspiring rogue states seeking a deterrent against future American military intervention against themselves.

Nature, Duration, and Scale of the War.

The American phase of the Vietnam War[6] began as a rural, peasant-based, materially self-sustaining Communist insurgency in the South waged by the National Liberation Front (NLF) against U.S.-supported South Vietnamese governmental infrastructure and security forces, and ended up primarily as a conventional military clash between U.S. and North Vietnamese regular forces (the People's Army of Vietnam, or PAVN). In contrast, Operation IRAQI FREEDOM began as an overwhelming U.S. conventional military operation that quickly crushed Iraq's regular forces and ended up as counterinsurgent campaign against Ba'athist regime remnants and their terrorist allies.

In Vietnam, the Communists waged a classic, centrally-directed, three-stage Maoist-model revolutionary war complete with territorial sanctuaries and a detailed political and economic program designed to mobilize peasant support. The Communists had a perfected strategy of revolutionary war, well-indoctrinated and –trained troops and political cadre, and a wealth of revolutionary war experience in the French-Indochinese War (1946-54). The Communist war in Vietnam also enjoyed critical external assistance.

The insurgency in Iraq bears little resemblance to this model.

Largely urban-based and relatively small in number, the Iraqi insurgents appear to be a mélange of former Ba'athist regime operatives, sympathetic Sunni Arabs (including disbanded Iraqi military officers and soldiers), al-Qaeda and other Islamist suicide bombers, hired gunmen and more recently militant anti-American Shi'ites. As such, the insurgency does not seem to be centrally directed the way the Vietnamese Communists were. The insurgency also has no declared agenda--a function probably of its disparate composition, though implicit in the targets of insurgent attacks is the aim of driving the United States out of Iraq and destabilizing the country, perhaps on behalf of a restoration of Sunni Arab rule. Indeed, until very recently, the Iraqi insurgency rested mainly on the minority Sunni Arab community, whose members account for only 20-25 percent of the population (the remainder being Kurds and Shi'ite Arabs). Now the insurgency has expanded (at least temporarily) to include militant Shi'ites, but the Iraq situation still stands in stark contrast to Vietnam where a class--the peasantry, comprising 80 percent of the total population in 1965--formed the indigenous manpower pool from which the Communist insurgency recruited its forces.

In terms of duration of conflict, there is also--so far--no similarity between the Iraq and Vietnam wars. Operation IRAQI FREEDOM was initiated in March 2003, and U.S. counterinsurgency operations continue as of this writing (mid-April 2004). In Indochina, U.S.-supported and -advised South Vietnamese counterinsurgency operations began in the early 1960s and steadily expanded throughout the decade. In 1965 the United States initiated a sustained air war against North Vietnam and began introducing major ground combat units into South Vietnam. The United States continued to conduct military operations in Indochina until January 1973, when it signed the Paris Peace Accord formally terminating further U.S. combat participation. Thus, for the United States the major combat phase of the Vietnam War lasted eight years (1965 through 1972).

The disparity between the two wars is even greater when it comes to scale. There is simply no comparison in forces committed and losses sustained. In terms of the former, U.S. military personnel deployed in South Vietnam peaked at 543,000 in April 1969; this force included nine U.S. Army and Marine Corps divisions plus selected subdivisional combat units. An additional 87,000 U.S. military personnel in Southeast Asia outside Vietnam supported in-country forces. Third country allied forces (supplied by Australia, South Korea, New Zealand, the Philippines, and Thailand), including two South Korean divisions, deployed in South Vietnam peaked in late 1968 at 65,000 troops. In that same year, the South Vietnamese armed forces fielded 820,000 troops (a number that grew to over one million by 1972).[7]

Communist troops in the Vietnam War, including regular PAVN personnel in the North and South and NLF (also known as Viet Cong, or VC) personnel in the South, numbered 300,000 in 1963, 700,000 in 1966, and almost one million in 1973.[8] On the eve of the strategically decisive Tet Offensive of 1968, Communist troops in South Vietnam alone, excluding self-defense militia, other part-time paramilitary, and political cadre, numbered between 250,000 and 300,000, of which 84-85,000 conducted the offensive (losing in the process 45-54,000 dead).[9] By comparison, the enemy in Iraq is numerically small, with insurgent Sunni Arab fighters estimated at no more than 5,000, not counting individuals performing noncombat tasks and passive and active political sympathizers.[10] Militant Shi'ites, both formally and loosely associated with the Muqtada al-Sadr movement and his Mahdi Army, may on the other hand number up to at least a few thousand fighters. It is unclear if this force will be able to exploit its conflict with coalition forces to increase its numbers or instead will be wiped out as a result of its challenge to the coaltion.

The Vietnam War, unlike the Iraq War, also had a huge and protracted aerial bombing component. Indeed, air operations in Indochina consumed about one-half of all U.S. war expenditure and consisted of sustained land- and sea-based bombing operations in South Vietnam, over Laos, and against North Vietnam. From 1962 to 1973, the U.S. Air Force tactical aircraft flew a total of almost 550,000 combat sorties in South Vietnam alone.[11] In terms of bomb tonnage dropped, it was the largest air war in history. During the 1962-73 period, tonnage dropped throughout Indochina totaled almost 8,000,000 tons, compared to the 1,235,000 tons dropped by Anglo-American bomber forces in the European theater during World War II.[12] (Additionally, U.S. ground forces in South Vietnam expended almost 7,000,000 tons of munitions compared to 3,600,000 in World War II.[13])

U.S. aircraft and air crew losses due to hostile action and accidents, though not in the same league as World War II, were also staggering, in large part because of North Vietnam's robust and technologically sophisticated Soviet-supplied air defenses and the unusual vulnerability of helicopters in South Vietnam's tactical settings. From 1962 to 1973, theater-wide U.S. aircraft losses, including helicopters, totaled 8,588, including 2,251 fixed-wing planes, and 2,700 airmen killed in action, not including helicopter crews; another 1,800 airmen were captured and became prisoners-of-war in North Vietnam.[14]

In Iraq, U.S. air power comprised a large component of the initial phase of major combat operations and enjoyed two great advantages over U.S. air operations against Vietnam: an enemy that lacked a functioning air force and effective air defenses, and the availability of plentiful quantities of precision strike munitions that maximized air-to-ground effectiveness at minimal human and political cost in collateral damage. As in Vietnam, however, helicopters proved vulnerable to small arms, machine guns, and hand-held missile and grenade launchers. During the major combat phase of the war (March 20-May 1), Iraqi gunfire downed one Apache helicopter (its two-man crew was captured) and struck another 30 helicopters. In a March 24 encounter near Karbala, Iraqi fire prompted the ordered withdrawal of elements of the 11th Aviation Regiment.[15]

So far, during the insurgent phase of the war, enemy fire and accidents have claimed a total of eight U.S. helicopters, and shoulder-fired surface-to-air missiles (SAMs) have damaged three fixed-wing transport aircraft.[16] Helicopter losses are likely to continue and could increase because Iraqi reliance on roadside bomb attacks encourages greater U.S. reliance on helicopters; rocket-propelled grenades are ubiquitous in Iraq; and it is believed that insurgent forces are acquiring advanced SA-16 and even SA-18 missile systems.[17]

U.S. Manpower Loss Rates.

During the 8 years of major U.S. combat operations in the Vietnam War--1965 through 1972, the United States suffered a total of 55,750 dead and 292,000 wounded, which translate into loss rates of 6,968 dead/36,600 wounded *per year*, 134/703 *per week*, and 19/100 *per day*.[18] These loss rates are well below those sustained in World War I (108 dead per day), World War II (305 per day), and the Korean War (48 dead per day), but considerably above those of the 1991 Gulf War (7 dead per day) and--so far--Operation IRAQI FREEDOM and its aftermath (in flux at about 1.5 - 2.0 per day at the time of this writing).[19]

On May 1, when President George W. Bush declared the termination of major U.S. combat operations, U.S. military forces had suffered a total of 138 battle and nonbattle deaths in Iraq.[20] These losses were later eclipsed by post-May 1, 2003, casualties. By mid-April 2004, U.S. casualties had reached 685 dead and over 3,000 wounded.[21]

The issue is whether these losses in Iraq are politically sustainable over time, a subject discussed below. In the Vietnam War, the Tet Offensive, although a major military setback for the Communists, undermined confidence within the Johnson administration that the enemy could be defeated soon and at an acceptable cost in American blood. Accordingly, the administration and its Nixon administration successor halted additional force deployments to Vietnam, entered into negotiations with the Communists, dropped insistence on withdrawal of North Vietnamese from South Vietnam as a component of a peace settlement, and began a series of unilateral U.S. troop withdrawals to reduce American casualties in Vietnam, which dropped dramatically from 1969 on.

The Enemy.

The enemy in the Vietnam War was numerically impressive, but then so too were peak-strength U.S. and South Vietnamese forces. Indeed, taken together, U.S., South Vietnamese, and third-country allied forces considerably outnumbered Communist forces. U.S. forces also enjoyed, as they did in 2003 in Iraq, an immense firepower advantage over the enemy. In the end, however, the United States abandoned South Vietnam to the Communists. Why?

The conventional explanation for U.S. defeat is that it was self-inflicted by some combination of civilian intrusion on U.S. military operations, a hostile media, and a large domestic anti-war movement. This judgment is not necessarily wrong as it is incomplete. For one thing, it ignores shortcomings in the U.S. military's performance within the political limitations imposed on the employment of force. More importantly, it ignores the enemy's performance; after all, the Sioux had something to do with General George Armstrong Custer's destruction along the Little Big Horn.[22]

A key to understanding the outcome of the Vietnam War as well as the outcome of many other conflicts in which the objectively weaker side prevails over the stronger (e.g., the American War of Independence, the Spanish *guerrilla* against Napoleon, the French-Indochinese War, the Soviet war in Afghanistan) is asymmetry of stakes.[23] If the Vietnamese conflict was a limited war for the United States, it was a total war for the Vietnamese Communists; and if the United States curbed the employment of its military power in Indochina, it grossly underestimated the "fighting power" (as Israeli military historian Martin van Creveld has used the term[24]) of the Communists, especially their willingness to die. Because the war was about national reunification, independence, and who would govern Vietnam, it could never have been remotely as important to the United States as it was to those Vietnamese who had been fighting since 1946 to rid Vietnam of foreign rule and influence. And nowhere was the Communists' superior will to prevail more evident than in the astounding casualties they were prepared to--and did-- incur.

In April 1995 the government in Hanoi announced that Communist forces during the "American period" of the Vietnam War had sustained a loss of 1,100,000 dead, a figure that presumably included the Communists' 300,000 missing in action. (Hanoi also estimated 2,000,000 civilian dead.)[25] The military dead represented 5 percent of the Communist population base during the Vietnam War of 20,000,000 (16,000,000 in North Vietnam and 4,000,000 in those areas of South Vietnam effectively controlled by the Communists). No other major belligerent in a 20th century war sustained such a high military death toll proportional to its population.[26] Another way of putting the 5 percent loss in perspective: it would equal about 15 million dead from the current U.S. population of almost 300,000,000. (The 600,000 total military dead in the American Civil War, by far the deadliest of all of America's wars, represented but 1.9 percent of the nation's 1860 population of 31,000,000.)[27]

Richard K. Betts comments on the effects of the "fundamental asymmetry on national interests" at stake in Vietnam:

> The Vietnamese Communists were fighting for their country
> as well as their principles, while the Americans had only
> principles at stake--and as the antiwar case became steadily
> more persuasive, even those principles were discredited. The
> only possibility for decisive victory for the United States lay
> in the complete obliteration of North Vietnam, an alternative
> unthinkably barbaric, unimaginably dangerous, and pointless.
> Hanoi bent but never broke because it preferred endless war to
> defeat; Washington bent and finally did break because the public
> preferred defeat to endless war.[28]

The insurgent enemy in Iraq is smaller in number, less ideologically and organizationally cohesive, and has no counterpart to North Vietnam, China, and the Soviet Union. Indeed, the Sunni Arab-based portion of the insurgency appeared tough but militarily manageable by U.S. and growing Iraqi security forces prior to Shi'ite cleric Muqtada al-Sadr's uprising which, at the time of this writing, appears worrisome but has not actually proven its staying power. Most insurgencies fail, especially if denied external assistance. That said, the insurgency's manageability could dramatically change if significant segments of Iraq's majority Shi'ite population rally to radical elements within their community and take up arms against U.S. forces. The April 2004 uprising of politically radicalized Shi'ites in Baghad, Kufa, Najaf, and other cities in southern Iraq killed dozens of U.S. troops and now threatens to open a Shi'ite front in what until then had been a primarily Sunni-based insurgency.[29]

In the early stages of the Iraqi insurgency, the most important and dangerous enemy elements were clearly Ba'athist regime remnants apparently fighting to restore some semblance of the old Saddamist order. The enemy's identity has since seemed to be changing with the increasing appearance of anti-American Islamic militants in the struggle with coalition forces and their Iraqi collaborators. In January 2004 the Central Intelligence Agency's (CIA) Deputy Director claimed that over 90 percent of the insurgents were Ba'ath Party loyalists, with the remainder being jihadists.[30] This judgment was probably true at the time, though since then the jihadist component seems to have grown relative to the Ba'athist component. In a February 12 interview, Lieutenant General Ricardo Sanchez, commander of U.S. forces in Iraq, stated that religious extremists and foreign fighters were beginning to supplant Ba'athist remnants as the primary members of the insurgency, a judgment seemingly validated by growing insurgent use of suicide and other types of bombings.[31] The Ba'athists and the Islamists may also be working to establish a level of operational cooperation that would make both groups more effective in opposing the coalition and its Iraqi collaborators.

The leadership of Iraq's insurgency remains unclear. Certainly there is no Iraqi insurgent equivalent of the charismatic Ho Chi Minh or the military mastermind Vo Nguyen Giap. The insurgency's continuation after Saddam Hussein's capture on December 13, 2003, strongly suggests that he was not playing a major role in its direction before then, notwithstanding the periodic release of audiotapes of Saddam calling upon Iraqis to wage a holy war against coalition forces.

Insurgent groups associated with the Ba'athists include the Return Party and Mohammed's Army. The former is known for mounting attacks on U.S. forces and distributing leaflets warning Iraqis not to cooperate with U.S. authorities. Mohammed's Army is a group apparently composed of former Iraqi intelligence and security agents; it has also attacked U.S. forces and issued leaflets vowing to take over cities vacated by coalition forces.[32] Additionally, an unknown number of criminals and unemployed former soldiers have been hired by the Ba'athists to engage in attacks on coalition forces for pay.

The Ba'athist insurgents may also have a large number of sympathizers and potential recruits among the Sunni Arab community in Iraq. Despite Saddam Hussein's abysmal record on human rights, many Sunni Arabs regarded him as a strong protector of their community, and even those Sunni Arabs who disliked Saddam have the least to gain from a genuinely democratic Iraq in which the country's Shi'ite majority, long the victim of Sunni Arab persecution, would exercise political power commensurate with its numbers. Moreover, high unemployment in the Sunni Arab areas, resentment over U.S. raids, the nature and scope of de-Ba'athification, and a lack of non-Ba'athist Sunni Arab leadership (except tribal chieftains) all contribute to potential Sunni Arab sympathy with the insurgents.[33]

If the Ba'athists still account for most insurgent fighters, the Islamists and foreign fighters may be the most threatening for Iraq's future. Saddam Hussein's overthrow brought foreign terrorists into Iraq and gave them a freedom of movement that was previously unthinkable. Under Saddam's regime, a pervasive and effective internal security apparatus blocked any serious insurgent activity, and 8 years of war with the Islamic Republic of Iran eliminated any potential sympathy Saddam might have had for Islamic extremists no matter how anti-American they might be. Moreover, some of Saddam's most dedicated domestic enemies were Islamic radicals who engaged in anti-regime terrorism.

Foreign fighters are currently entering Iraq from Syria and Iran, countries that have been historic rivals. They are also believed to have infiltrated from Saudi Arabia, while some have traveled from Yemen. Their numbers are uncertain. Most estimates by U.S. officials suggest that in early 2004 there were fewer than 1,000, with less than 10 infiltrating per day, though some Iraqi officials reportedly believe the total inside Iraq could be as high as several thousand.[34] The quality of foreign fighters appears to vary substantially from skilled hard-core jihadists to restless and untrained youths.

The best known Islamist terrorist group in the country is Ansar al Islam (Partisans of Islam), which is predominately a Kurdish organization of limited appeal to Arab Iraqis, including Islamists. Ansar developed and flourished during the last years of Saddam Hussein's rule in the areas of Iraqi Kurdistan along the Iranian border that were beyond the regime's control. Before the Iraq War, Ansar was widely believed to have links to al Qaeda and to Iranian intelligence services. Saddam Hussein's intelligence agents were sometimes also linked to Ansar as part of Saddam's periodic efforts to play off Kurdish groups against one another.[35]

Ansar al Islam has grown stronger since Saddam's fall. According to Coalition Authority Administrator Paul Bremer, hundreds of Ansar fighters returned from exile in Iran, and Ansar may be willing to put aside its conflict with the Ba'ath in order to strike U.S. forces.[36] It is also a natural ally for any al Qaeda operatives in Iraq.

In addition to Ansar, al Qaeda is sometimes described as having a significant presence in Iraq, taking advantage of the political and security vacuum created by the abrupt and utter disintegration of Saddam Hussein's regime. Evidence of this presence is scattered but highly plausible. Abu Musab al Zarqawi, a Jordanian-born terrorist leader with suspected strong ties to al Qaeda operatives, is believed to be in Iraq and is the leading suspect in all of the major suicide bombings that have been conducted in that country.[37] Indeed, the ongoing effectiveness of suicide and other large-scale bombings is often viewed as strong evidence of al Qaeda or its affiliates conducting operations in Iraq. These attacks have targeted the Jordanian embassy, UN headquarters, Kurdish political parties, and recruiting centers for new Iraqi army and police recruits. None of these targets, however, are exclusively enemies of al Qaeda, and in some cases there are more likely enemies for such attacks. Nevertheless, the techniques of attack suggest Islamic extremists or those inspired by them.

An often overlooked insurgent component consists of individuals who seek personal revenge against occupation forces for previous actions against themselves or their families; anecdotal information from Iraq suggests that a number of insurgents fall into this category.[38] They may be individuals who lost family, including soldiers in the war itself, or individuals offended by U.S. troops during the occupation. The blood vendettas of the Arabs often are completely unforgiving in these circumstances.

Whatever their origins or motivations, it is also clear that Iraqi insurgent forces are nowhere nearly as capable as the Vietnamese Communists of the 1960s and early 1970s. Iraqi fighters often seem to favor soft targets, whereas the Vietnamese Communists were willing to take on large U.S. Army and Marine Corps combat units. The Communists were also organized into regimental- and divisional-size units, whereas Iraqi fighters seem to operate in groups no larger than squads. The Communists in South Vietnam also had large-scale external access to increasing quantities of ever more sophisticated weaponry that the Iraqi insurgents can only dream of. That said, the Iraqi insurgents are better armed today than were Communist insurgents in South Vietnam in the early 1960s, who at that time were compelled to rely largely on stolen, captured, and home-made weapons. As under Saddam Hussein, Iraq remains a heavily-armed society with weapons and ammunition available in abundance throughout the country.

Finally, unlike the Vietnamese Communists, the Iraqi insurgents have no apparent unifying ideology, strategy, or vision of a future Iraq. Their operations often appear decentralized and uncoordinated, and if they share the objective of forcing the Americans out of Iraq, it remains unclear that they have an agreed-upon strategy for doing so. Simply kill enough U.S. troops to undercut domestic American political support for a continued military presence in Iraq? Terrorize Iraqis away from cooperating in Iraq's political reconstruction? Foment a chaotic civil war in Iraq (complete with Iranian and perhaps Turkish intervention) beyond U.S. ability to control?

Military Operations.

In Vietnam, the United States waged two parallel albeit overlapping wars: an attritional ground war in the South and a coercive air war against the North. Both ultimately failed.

In the South, the U.S. Military Command, Vietnam (MACV), concluded that prohibition of ground force operations in Laos and across the Vietnamese Demilitarized Zone left it no alternative to waging a war of attrition against Communist forces inside South Vietnam itself. The MACV believed that American firepower could inflict intolerable casualties on the Communists, that it could force the enemy beyond a "cross-over point" or "breaking point" at which he could no longer replace his losses. The strategy, however, ignored the Communists' demonstrated tenacity and capacity for sacrifice as well as their substantial manpower pool. More importantly, the strategy mistakenly assumed that U.S. forces would have the initiative, more often than not forcing the enemy to fight on U.S. terms. In fact, it was the Communists, not the Americans, who initiated 70-80 percent of all firefights, which meant that they could control their losses by, among other things, refusing combat altogether when it suited them to do so.[39] Observed Douglas Blaufarb:

> By and large, then--and this is the essence of the [VC/PAVN's] ability to survive in the teeth of American superiority--the enemy was able to control the pace and scope of combat and thus the level of combat losses by evading contact when it did not suit his purpose. By this means, he managed to keep losses within his capacity to replace them, even despite the length of his supply and replacement lines and his lack of mobility and heavy firepower. Generally alerted in advance to American intentions, he avoided battle until he was ready. To him, losses--at least up to a high level never actually reached--did not matter, terrain did not matter. What mattered was to keep the force in being, its morale

high, and its minimum supply requirements assured — and to exact a price from the Americans which in the long run would be felt painfully.[40]

Counting enemy bodies on the battlefield (even had the process not been corrupted) thus counted for nothing as a measure of strategic success as long as those bodies were replaceable.

To be sure, the Communists incurred terrible losses when, as in their Tet Offensive of 1968 and Easter Offensive of 1972, they tried to take and hold fixed positions against U.S. firepower. But this behavior was exceptional. At no time did the MACV come close to pushing the Communists to their manpower breaking point. On the contrary, it was the Communists who forced to Americans to their manpower breaking point; by 1968, additional U.S. force deployments would have necessitated a massive Reserve call-up, which President Johnson refused to contemplate.

The attrition strategy and its attendant search for high body counts also encouraged a less than discriminating employment of firepower in Vietnam's rural areas that produced substantial levels of collateral damage that hardly endeared the peasantry to the South Vietnamese government. Much of the countryside was destroyed or otherwise rendered untenable, creating a burgeoning flow of refugees to urban areas where they found little in the way of housing or gainful employment. Precision-guided weapons were then in their infancy, to be sure; that said, however, the elevation of the body-count as the sole measure of battlefield success offered no incentive to be discriminating.

The air war against North Vietnam also rested on an underestimation of Hanoi's will to win and capacity to absorb punishment. As a pre-industrial totalitarian state, North Vietnam was a poor candidate for defeat through air power. It was also, thanks largely to Soviet advice and generous military assistance, capable of imposing significant costs on attacking American aircraft. Unlike Iraq in 2003, North Vietnam had a small but effective fighter interceptor force, a powerful and integrated air defense system, and a significant capacity for rapid bomb damage repair--especially of its critical railroad network. Hanoi also profited from repeated U.S. bombing pauses undertaken for diplomatic reasons and, with respect to Operation ROLLING THUNDER (1965-68), a gradualist application of U.S. air power that permitted North Vietnam to adapt its defenses and tactics. U.S. air losses in North Vietnam totaled 925 fixed-wing aircraft from 1966 through early 1973.[41]

Factors other than the enemy and political constraints on the use of force adversely affected U.S. military performance. Aside from the inherent limitations of American conventional military power in the revolutionary war setting of Indochina, there was no unified command of the war. Goldwater-Nichols was 20 years in the future. There was no joint warfare in Vietnam; on the contrary, inter-service rivalry dominated, producing disunity of command and precluding the provision of timely and useful military advice to civilian authority. The Joint Chiefs of Staff were joint in name only; they served up conflicting advice, lowest-common-denominator advice, or no advice at all. H. R. McMaster comments on the crucial decisionmaking period of mid-1964 to mid-1965:

> [E]ach of the services, rather than attempt to determine the true nature of the war and the source of the insurgency in South Vietnam, assumed that it alone had the capacity to win the war. The Air Force believed that bombing North Vietnam and interdicting infiltration routes could solve the problem of insurgency in the South. . . . The Army viewed increased American involvement in Vietnam in the context of a protracted commitment of ground forces and believed that bombing the North might intensify the war in the South. . . . [The Marines] advocate[d] bombing as only the first step in a larger program that included the introduction of large numbers of Marines into South Vietnam to establish secure "enclaves" along the coast.[42]

Service parochialism was especially pronounced in the organization and conduct of air operations. Air operations in Indochina were fragmented across four commands: the Strategic Air Command (Omaha, Nebraska), 7th Air Force (Saigon), the Pacific Command (Honolulu), and 13th Air Force (Philippines). Additionally, the U.S. ambassador in Laos exercised a veto over any proposed air operations in that country. Air operations against North Vietnam were divvied up into seven "route packages," three farmed out to the Air Force and four to the Navy.[43] After the war, former 7th Air Force Commander William Momyer conceded that the route package system "compartmentalized our air power and reduced its capabilities and inevitably prevented a unified concentrated air effort."[44] Henry Kissinger concluded that the "bizarre way the air campaign was organized throughout the war told more about the Pentagon's bureaucracy than about military realities; indeed, it showed that Washington's organizational requirements overrode strategy."[45]

The MACV's manpower policies were no less debilitating to military effectiveness on the ground. Rotational tours of duty of 1 year for enlisted personnel and 3-6 months for officers, though important to morale (especially to conscripted and draft-induced "volunteers"), sapped small unit cohesion under fire and compromised the ability of officers and men alike to accumulate and sustain knowledge of and skill in fighting the strange war in which Americans found themselves in Vietnam. "In and out like clockwork . . . just long enough to figure out what they didn't know," observed combat veteran David Hackworth.[46] Westmoreland's concern for troop morale and his reliance on massive firepower to "attrit" the enemy also fostered very high ratios of support to combat troops, which undermined the potential military productivity of the half-million troops he was granted to fight the war. For considerations of morale, huge base camp facilities were constructed, complete with movie theaters, swimming pools, snack shops, ice cream factories, slot machines, steam baths, baseball diamonds, post offices, and lawns. To maximize firepower and supporting logistics, the MACV authorized construction in South Vietnam of seven jet-capable and 75 smaller airfields, six deep water ports, and dozens of huge warehouse complexes.[47]

The result was that, by 1968, no more than 80,000--or 15 percent--of the 536,000 U.S. military personnel in Vietnam were actually available for sustained ground combat operations; indeed, less than 10 percent of the total of 2,800,000 Americans who served in what was first and foremost an infantry war served in line infantry units.[48] Given the high fat content of U.S. forces and the relatively low tail-to-teeth ratio of the Communist side, the MACV was probably outnumbered in effective soldiers. Communist forces were leaner because they relied more on stealth and cunning than firepower, and because they recruited hundreds of thousands of peasant coolies to perform logistical tasks. They also lived in the field, as had U.S. forces in World War II and Korea. Bruce Palmer, Jr., one of Westmoreland's deputies, believed the base-camp idea was even worse than the 1-year tour for enlisted men: "The manpower it soaked up was appalling, not to mention the waste of material resources and the handicap of having to defend and take care of these albatrosses."[49]

The Vietnamese Communists, for their part, brought to the battlefield not only a superior will, but also a strategy dictated by their materiel inferiority and dedicated to exploiting the Americans' inferior will. Revolutionary war as they practiced it was a weapon for the seizure of political power from a militarily superior foe; it was designed for insurgent groups in pre-industrial states seeking to overthrow foreign rule or neocolonial governments.

Vietnamese revolutionary war, which drew heavily on Chinese Communist theory and practice, combined mass political mobilization of the peasantry and a reliance on guerrilla tactics that deprived a firepower superior conventional foe of decisive targets to shoot at. The keys to success were elusiveness and protraction. The presence of a firepower-superior enemy mandated refusal to present decisive targets, which in turn dictated avoidance of pitched battles, heavy reliance on camouflage and night operations, hit-and-run attacks, and use of terrain and populations as means of concealment. The fact that Communist forces sometimes violated these tactics to their great loss simply underscores their effectiveness. Nor does the Communists' turn to primary reliance on conventional military operations in the early 1970s invalidate the utility of revolutionary war as a weapon against the Americans. Communist revolutionary war doctrine anticipated such operations in the final stage of conflict. More to the point, the purpose of pre-conventional military operations was to weaken the enemy's will through protraction of hostilities, which is exactly what the Communists succeeded in doing during the 3 years of major combat operations culminating in the Tet Offensive.

Protraction essentially pitted time against American materiel superiority. Protraction played, as it had against the French in the First Indochina War, to the inherent impatience of Western democracies with costly and seemingly interminable wars waged on behalf of interests ultimately regarded as less compelling than those at stake for Vietnamese Communism. For the Communists, there was no alternative to protraction because a swift victory over the Americans was impossible. Protraction was thus both politically and militarily imperative. And it worked.

In Iraq, the U.S. leadership did not seem to expect protracted irregular warfare beyond the termination of major combat operations. As liberator of all Iraqis from a brutal tyranny, U.S. forces, it was widely believed, would be as welcomed in Iraq as had been Anglo-American and Free French forces in France in 1944.[50] Some argue that the prospect of guerrilla warfare was dismissed because, among other things, it raised the prospect of a Vietnam-like quagmire. Frank official discussion of possible intractable postwar political and military challenges in Iraq would have impeded efforts to mobilize public support for going to war.

Insurgent attacks in Iraq have been directed at a variety of targets, including U.S. and coalition troops, American civilian contractors, Iraqis working with Americans, and oil and electrical power infrastructure. Moreover, just as the Viet Cong targeted South Vietnamese government officials in the 1960s, Iraqi insurgents have attacked members of the Interim Governing Council (assassinating two of them at the time of this writing), mayors and other local Iraqi politicians, police stations and police officers, and members of the New Iraqi Army and other security forces.

Insurgent tactics have evolved over time as the various groups have engaged in trial and error. They include ambushes with small arms and especially rocket-propelled grenades, use of improvised explosive devises (IEDs), shoot-and-scoot mortar attacks, and vehicle and other types of bombings. IEDs are the weapons most frequently used against U.S. and coalition forces, while car bombs are more often directed against softer targets, including New Iraqi Army and police force units and individuals. As of early February 2004, almost 400 IEDs were reported to have exploded near U.S. convoys traveling Iraqi roads, and more than 2,500 had been discovered and disarmed. Many IEDs are mortar and artillery shells, some of them strung together, and most are very well-camouflaged.[51]

Iraqi police officers and other security forces are special targets because they are viewed as successors to eventually withdrawn U.S. forces. They are also more vulnerable because they carry less lethal weaponry than U.S. troops, suffer tactical communications difficulties, receive limited and hasty training in force protection, and often lack body armor and even lightly armored vehicles. Translators and even laundresses working for Americans are also targeted for the purpose of deterring other Iraqis from serving the Coalition Provisional Authority and U.S. forces.[52]

Pacification.

One of the ironies of the Vietnam War is that the original southern-rooted insurgency that prompted U.S. military intervention in the first place was significantly pacified--though by no means extirpated--by the time the last major U.S. ground combat forces departed South Vietnam. The magnitude and destructiveness of U.S. intervention imposed manpower losses upon NLF forces that were unsustainable without increased assistance from regular PAVN forces. The turning point was the 1968 Tet Offensive, which was conducted primarily by NLF forces with PAVN units held in reserve (except at Khe Sanh). The NLF incurred horrendous losses taking and attempting to hold towns and cities against massive U.S. firepower delivered with perfunctory regard for avoiding collateral damage. During the half-decade separating the Tet Offensive and the fall of Saigon, PAVN regulars--as both formed units and as individual fillers in remaining NLF formations--came to dominate the Communist military effort. By 1972, a conflict that had begun as an indigenous guerrilla war against the Saigon regime had evolved into a conventional military contest between the U.S. and regular North Vietnamese forces.

NLF manpower losses on behalf of a manifest military failure not only depressed recruiting but also prompted unprecedented defections to the Government of Vietnam (GVN) side. But the shock of Tet alone was not enough to pacify the insurgency. Tet initially disrupted pacification, but it also galvanized the MACV and the GVN to undertake long-contemplated measures that crippled the insurgency by 1973 but failed to counter the burgeoning Communist conventional military threat. Even before the Tet Offensive, the United States had undertaken a complete reorganization of its pacification efforts, which had been scattered across a host of agencies, accorded low priority, and lacked any unified strategy. In 1967, with strong presidential backing, pacification was granted heightened priority, and pacification activities were centralized and coordinated under

Civilian Operations and Revolutionary Development Support (CORDS) headed by a civilian deputy to the MACV for pacification and administered through interagency civil-military advisory teams at the national, regional, provincial, and district levels.[53] The effect was a major boost of resources dedicated to pacification and their much more efficient and effective administration. CORDS provided advice, assistance, and training across virtually the entire portfolio of normal government functions, as well as such war tasks as training village militia and provincial paramilitary forces and funding and advising a national program to encourage Communist defectors and reintegrate them into society.

CORDS took advantage of the temporary political vacuum the Tet Offensive had created in the countryside to move back into the villages with an Accelerated Pacification Program (APC) carried out by U.S.-advised South Vietnamese Revolutionary Development cadre teams supported by dedicated U.S. military operations. Beginning in November 1968 and continuing through the end of 1971, the percentage of South Vietnam's rural population under effective government control steadily increased, especially in the Mekong Delta. According to perhaps the definitive assessment of U.S. pacification efforts in South Vietnam, "the APC marked the start of a period, roughly 1969 to early 1972, of uninterrupted gains in population security throughout South Vietnam and further erosion of the Viet Cong."[54]

A major reason, aside from Tet losses, why the strength of VC guerrilla units dropped from 77,000 to 25,000 during the period January 1968 to May 1972[55] was the GVN's belated decision to mobilize fully its available manpower for military and paramilitary service, which had the effect of drying up much of the manpower pool from which the VC recruited.[56] Making matters worse for the guerrillas were GVN decisions to restore traditional political autonomy to villages (taken away by the regime Ngo Dinh Diem) and to create village militias (People's Self Defense Forces). But perhaps the greatest blow to the VC's political fortunes among the peasantry was the sweeping land reform Saigon finally enacted in 1970 (the Land to the Tiller program), which redistributed 2.5 million acres of landlord controlled land free to approximately two-thirds of the tenant farmers in South Vietnam (the GVN compensated the landlords).[57]

Pacification initiatives did not, however, destroy the VC's network of political cadre in South Vietnam, known as the Viet Cong Infrastructure (VCI). Though thousands of political operatives died in battle and though the controversial Phoenix Program targeted the VCI, the VCI retained its structural integrity, albeit at substantially reduced strength and quality, by recruiting and training new cadre in South Vietnam and bringing in more from the North.[58] Indeed, one of the very negative trends in South Vietnam during the post-Tet years was a significant increase in VC terrorist attacks on local government officials and civilians participating in government pacification programs, with civilian casualties in 1969 and 1970 alone averaging 26,000.[59]

It is nevertheless fair to say that by the time the Paris Peace Accord was signed, the Viet Cong insurgent element of the war--as opposed to PAVN's conventional military element--had been defeated to the point of being militarily peripheral, even irrelevant to the war's final outcome, given the PAVN's final offensive to come. This does not mean that South Vietnam, even had it been left alone by North Vietnam after the Paris Peace Accord--an impossible counterfactual if there ever was one, had already immunized itself from an existential insurgent threat. Despite genuine land reform, some progress toward democratic institutions, improved standards of living, and political stability in Saigon, pacification failed to create a genuine political community in South Vietnam[60] in large measure because it made no progress--it was not intended to--against the GVN's greatest weakness: rampant corruption.

Pacification in South Vietnam was directed against a classic, peasant-based, Maoist-model insurgency; as such, pacification efforts involved significant nonmilitary programs and initiatives aimed at swaying peasant loyalties away from the Communists and toward the GVN. No such insurgency or pacification program exists in Iraq. The mélange of disparate groups that comprise the smaller and until recently largely Sunni Arab and urban-based insurgency in Iraq has no national political program, makes no pretense of competing for the loyalty of most Iraqis, and seems much less selective than the Vietnamese Communists in the use of high-collateral damage tactics and weaponry.

These features of the Iraqi insurgency, together with the absence of the kind of powerful external allies the Vietnamese Communists enjoyed, have led to an approach to pacification emphasizing "sticks" over "carrots" when dealing with proven supporters of the insurgency. Because the overthrow of Saddam Hussein ended centuries of Sunni political domination of Iraq and its predecessor entities, and because the restoration of that dominance would be impossible in any genuinely representative new government, there is little in the way of political "carrots" that the Coalition Political Authority or its Iraqi successor could offer as a means of "pacifying" Sunni Arab hardliners. The "carrots" that can be offered center on material aid, efforts to keep Sunni Arabs employed, and more sweepingly a limited tolerance of Sunni militias in places such as Baghdad that could serve as a reassurance against bullying by a Shi'ite-dominated government.

Accordingly, U.S. forces have relied heavily on "sticks" in Sunni Arab strongholds. In an effort to break the insurgency, those forces have conducted numerous raids into potentially hostile areas with the aim of arresting suspected insurgents, finding documents of intelligence value, seizing illegal weapons and explosives--and in so doing, crippling the insurgency's ability to continue attacking coalition forces and reconstruction targets.[61]

The success of raiding remains unclear. Suspects have been arrested, and weapons and valuable documents seized. Raids can, however, alienate innocent people swept up in them or offended by the terrifying surprise intrusion of foreign troops in private family settings. The employment of attack aircraft as a weapon of counterinsurgency in Iraq[62] certainly risks the kind of overkill that impeded U.S. pacification efforts in South Vietnam. Additionally, the de-Ba'athification campaign in Iraq is widely viewed within the Sunni community as callous and excessive, going far beyond simply punishing the collaborators and henchmen of the Saddam Hussein regime.[63] Within the conspiracy-minded Middle East, a variety of Iraqi Sunnis believe the United States favors a Shi'ite-dominated Iraqi government which will be a source of ongoing repression of the Sunni. This belief is widely held among Arab elites in neighboring states. Necessary U.S. efforts to reassure Iraq's Shi'ites are often misinterpreted by Iraq's Sunni Arabs as a policy of favoritism toward the Shi'ites.

As in Vietnam, moreover, the United States is finding it difficult to identify reliable measures of counterinsurgent success in Iraq.

Insurgent body counts (killed and captured) are unreliable if the insurgency can replace its losses; the supply of suicide bombers, for example, seems to be inexhaustible. Additionally, given the predominantly urban setting of the Iraqi insurgency, territorial control is a more or less meaningless measure of success.

Role of Allies.

In 1965 the United States did not bother to seek U.N. authorization for intervention in Vietnam because of the certainty of a Soviet veto. In 2003, the United States sought an authorizing resolution but failed to garner even a majority among the U.N. Security Council's membership. Indeed, in both cases, much of the rest of the world, including key allies, regarded U.S. military intervention as illegitimate, wrongheaded, or both. Not a single NATO ally joined the United States in Vietnam; on the contrary, notwithstanding the Johnson administration's obsession with the need for international allies to legitimize its war in Southeast Asia, only five other states aside from South Vietnam itself (Australia, New Zealand, the Philippines, South Korea, and Thailand) contributed combat troops to what were then called Free World Forces in Vietnam, and of the five, only one (South Korea) contributed a substantial force (50,000 men organized around two combat divisions).[64] Moreover, the Korean divisions were funded and equipped entirely by the United States, and they were contributed to South Vietnam as a substitute for the redeployment of U.S. forces from South Korea to South Vietnam.[65]

In its South Vietnamese ally, however, the United States enjoyed a significant asset that it lacks in Iraq: large, U.S.-trained and -equipped indigenous army and security forces capable of shouldering static defense and para-police functions nationwide, thereby releasing U.S. combat forces for other tasks. At its peak strength, the Army of the Republic of Vietnam (ARVN), by far the largest component of the Republic of Vietnam Armed Forces (RVNAF), which consisted of a national regular force of 13 divisions and more than a dozen independent elite units supplemented by separate forces maintained at the regional and provincial levels, numbered over 1,000,000 strong, or almost double peak-strength U.S. forces.[66] South Vietnam also had a sizeable air force (peak strength: 39 operational squadrons) and a navy (672 amphibious, 450 patrol, and over 300 other vessels).[67]

Notwithstanding the ARVN's numerical strength, two great weakness doomed it as a contestant against Vietnamese Communist forces both before and after U.S. major military intervention: a venal and professionally inferior senior officer corps, and a poorly trained and motivated soldiery. The United States decided to commit major combat forces to Vietnam in 1965 precisely because the ARVN was rapidly losing to Communist forces; a decade later, the ARVN, again fighting without assistance from U.S. combat forces, disintegrated in the face of the Communists' final offensive. "Vietnamization," the post-Tet Offensive U.S. program to simultaneously withdraw U.S. forces from Vietnam and expand and modernize the ARVN, was destined to fail absent U.S. military reintervention in the war because it assumed that the ARVN could succeed where the MACV had failed. The ARVN nonetheless accounted for considerable Communist dead; if the ARVN performed poorly on the offensive, many units often fought effectively on the defensive (for example, against the Communist Tet attacks), and its capacity for sacrifice was evident in the more than 250,000 dead it sustained during the decade leading up North Vietnam's final offensive.[68]

If America's allies in the Vietnam War were few and unimpressive by U.S. standards, the opposite was true for the Vietnamese Communists. Unlike Saddam Hussein's Iraq in 2003, the Communists in Vietnam had powerful and ultimately decisive allies. Behind the NLF in the South stood North Vietnam, and behind North Vietnam stood the Soviet Union and China. The Soviet Union supplied Hanoi 5-10 million metric tons of war materiel valued, depending on the method of calculation, between $3.6 and $11 billion (in then-year dollars); deliveries included several hundred fighter aircraft, thousands of antiaircraft guns and field artillery pieces, hundreds of surface-to-air missile batteries, thousands of tanks, helicopters, and military trucks, and huge amounts of infantry weapons and ammunition.[69] The Soviets also sent thousands of technical advisers to train the Vietnamese to operate the sophisticated weaponry the Soviets were supplying.

For their part, the Chinese, who had provided the Vietnamese Communists critical artillery and other materiel assistance in the French-Indochinese War, also delivered huge quantities of weapons and munitions to Hanoi. Unlike the Russians, however, the Chinese provided over 300,000 antiaircraft and engineer troops who, in the face of escalating U.S. bombing, manned air defense systems and constructed, reconstructed, maintained, and defended North Vietnam's transportation network, especially its railroad system.[70] This assistance not only released considerable Vietnamese manpower for other military tasks but also underscored the seriousness of Beijing's commitment to North Vietnam, which as we have seen was a sensitive point for President Lyndon Johnson, if not for his successor (who sought to engage China as a potential strategic partner against the Soviet Union).

In Iraq, as in Vietnam, the United States has sought international support both to reduce its military burden and to enhance the legitimacy of its policy, although it strongly resisted giving the United Nations a major voice in postwar Iraq policy. In Iraq, as in Vietnam, this effort produced disappointing results, although the number and variety of countries contributing forces to Iraq's postwar stabilization is much more impressive than those that sent troops to Vietnam. In both cases, the United States bore the primary manpower burden of the fighting, although in Vietnam, unlike Iraq, a large indigenous force performed important static defense and other military tasks.

In Iraq, invading U.S. ground forces numbered three divisions, a brigade combat team, and various support units for a total of more than 115,000 troops; the U.S. force presence in Iraq subsequently peaked at about 140,000 as reinforcements arrived and the mission shifted to stability operations. The most notable allied contribution came from the United Kingdom, which contributed 26,000 troops; Australia contributed an additional 2,000.[71]

Since the termination of major combat operations on May 1, 2003, a number of other countries, for a variety of motives, some of them having little to do with support for U.S. policy in Iraq, have committed limited force contingents to assist Iraq's postwar stabilization. Britain, not surprisingly, has maintained the largest force contingent after the United States, with 8,200 troops in Iraq as of March 2004.[72] British-commanded multinational forces in southern Iraq now include contingents from Italy (2,900), the Netherlands (1,060), Denmark (545), Romania (514), the Czech Republic (271),

Norway (129), Portugal (128), Lithuania (95), and New Zealand (55).[73]

Poland, which has 2,500 troops in Iraq, commands the south-central sector consisting of additional troops from Spain (1,300), Ukraine (1,000), Bulgaria (650, including police), El Salvador (380), Honduras (370), Dominican Republic (250), Nicaragua (250), Romania (230), Philippines (178, including police and civilians), Mongolia (171), Latvia (106), Slovakia (85), and Kazakhstan (27).[74]

By late February 2004, South Korea and Japan had also agreed to send troops to Iraq. Approximately 900 Australian troops are also deployed in and around Iraq.[75] Nicaragua sent 115 troops but withdrew them for financial reasons. Additionally, Thailand, Hungary, Azerbaijan, Albania, Georgia, Estonia, and Macedonia have sent noncombat contingents ranging in size from 28 to 400 troops.[76]

South Korea originally contributed 675 troops, but later agreed to provide another 3,000. These additional troops were scheduled to deploy to the northern city of Kirkuk by the end of April and were supposed to operate under their own command. In March 2004, however, Seoul cancelled the planned deployment to Kirkuk because of questionable security in the area and concern that its troops would have to participate in offensive military operations. South Korea emphasized that it still planned to deploy these troops in Iraq, but that the deployment was now expected to be delayed until June, when a new site for deployment could be determined.[77] The South Korean government continues to face strong domestic opposition to its military involvement in Iraq.

Japan, another major U.S. Asian ally, has sent approximately 1,000 troops to Iraq, where they are deployed to the southern city of Samawah in cooperation with the British and also to Baghdad International Airport. Japanese public opinion, though initially strongly opposed to deployment, had softened by March 2004, though it remains unclear how the Japanese public might react to casualties. Shintaro Ishihara, the governor of Tokyo, has stated the he expects that casualties will generate a surge of support for the government, although it would seem equally possible that many Japanese would reconsider the wisdom of sending troops to Iraq.[78]

The political staying power of key allied troop contributors remains uncertain, however, because their troop presence in Iraq generated domestic political controversy from the start. Many democratic governments sent troops against the wishes of public majorities back home, and domestic opposition groups have naturally latched on to popular discontent in efforts to challenge sitting governments. Opposition parties in Australia, Portugal, and the Netherlands have demanded official inquiries into governmental decisions to support the war, especially into what they believed about Iraq's WMD before the war was launched.[79] In Spain, 3 days after devastating al Qaeda bombings in Madrid that killed almost 200 people on March 11, 2004, the electorate voted into office a new government dedicated to withdrawing Spanish troops from Iraq and repudiating its predecessor government's unpopular strategic alignment with the United States. Indeed, the Madrid attacks underscore the homeland vulnerability of states contributing forces in Iraq and the potential political vulnerability of governments that, in following the United States into Iraq, have bucked the wishes of their domestic electorates.

Insurgent attacks on non-U.S. coalition forces in Iraq also may increase domestic political pressures on governments contributing contingents. Italian, Spanish, and Polish forces have already been attacked by car bombers. Unilateral withdrawal of several or more allied contingents could be a serious setback for U.S. Iraq policy because they usually do not draw the ire that U.S. forces do and because their contributing governments are not perceived to have imperialist agendas in Iraq. Additionally, the more "Americanized" the already heavily American foreign presence in Iraq becomes, the more likely it is that it will provoke increased Iraqi nationalist opposition. Some Iraqi nationalists may be drawn to the insurgent cause by what they view as a prolonged U.S. troop withdrawal and the continued absence of a new U.N. effort to take over the establishment of a new Iraq, The United Nations, for all of its shortcomings, has greater legitimacy in the Arab world than does the United States.

State-Building.

The Vietnam War ended as a war between two states, the northern Democratic Republic of Vietnam (DRV) and the southern Republic of Vietnam (RVN). Ho Chi Minh declared the former state established in September 1945, whereas the latter state was formed in 1954 on the basis of an antecedent French surrogate in the wake of the Geneva Accords that concluded the French Indochinese War and mandated the withdrawal of France from Indochina. Both states, separated by what was supposed to be a temporary dividing line along the 17th Parallel pending nationwide elections in 1956, claimed to be the sole legitimate government of all of Vietnam.

The United States supported the RVN from its inception as a bulwark against further Communist expansion in Southeast Asia; it is fair to say that but for U.S. political sponsorship and economic and military largesse, the anti-Communist regime of President Ngo Dinh Diem and his successors could have been neither created nor sustained. Indeed, the impending military collapse of South Vietnam in 1965 prompted major U.S. combat intervention, and the absence of that intervention a decade later doomed the U.S. Cold War client state.

The United States embraced state-building in South Vietnam for 2 decades. It fostered, advised, and funded governmental institutions and activities across the board; it armed and trained the RVN armed forces (RVNAF) and security services; it financed the RVN's war costs and subsidized South Vietnam's economy; and it attempted to guide the RVN toward adoption of democratic institutions. In the end, however, state-building failed. Why? The obvious answer is the RVN's military defeat in 1975. But this begs the question of why the RVN was defeated so quickly, surprising even the Communists, who expected their final offensive to take 2, even 3, years.[80] Why did the RVNAF, well-equipped and numerically strong, disintegrate in less than 2 months, with senior officers fleeing ahead of their men? Why did the RVNAF, which for all practical purposes *was* the South Vietnamese state by virtue of its monopoly of RVN administrative authority, fail to fight effectively for the non-Communist order it represented?

It is easy to blame United States. In the wake of the Tet Offensive, the United States reduced its principal war aim from securing an independent, non-Communist South Vietnam to seeking an honorable withdrawal; it then proceeded unilaterally to withdraw its combat troops from the fight, and in 1973 signed a treaty that barred their return while leaving the NVA undisturbed inside South Vietnam.[81] During this same period, in the name of "Vietnamization," the United States also funded the RVNAF's expansion and modernization well beyond the RVN's capacity to man and maintain it. And when the final Communist offensive was launched in 1975, the United States failed not only to re-enter the war but also to provide the materiel assistance (mostly replacement equipment, ammunition, and spare parts) Saigon desperately requested in the wake of the ARVN's abandonment of massive weapons and equipment in its pell-mell retreat from the Central Highlands.

But none of this excuses the RVN from some share--in our view, the primary share--of responsibility for its demise. In its life-and-death struggle with the DRV, the RVN was crippled from the start by three main weaknesses that no amount of American intervention could offset: professional military inferiority, rampant corruption, and lack of political legitimacy.[82] Joseph Buttinger, a renowned scholar of Vietnamese history and society, concluded in the wake of South Vietnam's destruction that:

> The swift and dramatic collapse of the South Vietnamese army and the Saigon regime was not the result of an overwhelming attack by superior military forces. It came about because of the degree of moral disintegration the South Vietnamese army had reached in 1975. This in turn reflected the degree of moral and political decay to which South Vietnamese society had sunk after years of increasing political terror, mass misery and corruption. Moral disintegration alone can explain why an army three times the size and possessing more than five times the equipment of the enemy could be as rapidly defeated as the ARVN was between March 10 and April 30, 1975.[83]

Cao Van Vien, the RVNAF's last Chief of Staff, described a domino doomed to fall by 1975:

> South Vietnam was approaching political and economic bankruptcy. National unity no longer existed; no one was able to rally the people behind the national cause. Riddled by corruption and sometimes ineptitude and dereliction, the government hardly responded to the needs of a public which had gradually lost confidence in it. . . . Under these conditions, the South Vietnamese social fabric gradually disintegrated, influenced in part by mistrust, divisiveness, uncertainty, and defeatism until the whole nation appeared to resemble a rotten fruit ready to fall at the first passing breeze.[84]

From the RVN's inception in 1955 until its collapse 20 years later, its leadership failed to create a military establishment of sufficient integrity and competence to give as good as it got from the PAVN and Viet Cong. If the RVNAF enjoyed a numerical and firepower advantage over its Communist foe, it suffered--before, during, and after the war's Americanization--a decided inferiority in the intangibles that make up genuine fighting power. With some notable exceptions, RVNAF units were poorly led and motivated, and in great contrast to both Communist and U.S. combat forces, did not seek contact with the enemy. The RVNAF was also, again with notable exceptions, corrupt, from the chicken-stealing private to the kickback-receiving province chief, and, by most accounts, thoroughly penetrated by Communist agents.[85] A 1967 State Department assessment of the RVNAF concluded that it suffered from poor leadership, poor morale, poor relations with the population, and

> low operational capabilities including poor coordination, tactical rigidity, overdependence on air and artillery support arising in part from inadequate firepower, overdependence on vehicular convoy, unwillingness to remain in the field at night or over adequately long periods, and lack of aggressiveness.[86]

The conventionality of the RVNAF's force structure, widely criticized as unsuited for the challenges posed by Communist revolutionary war, probably did not really matter in the long run. The effectiveness of any force structure hinges upon the professional ability of its officer corps to lead and upon the willingness of its soldiery to be led, and the RVNAF proved fatally deficient in both respects. The RVNAF was as incapable of dealing with the Communists' conventional offensive of 1975 as it was with the Communist insurgency of the early 1960s.

The sources of the RVNAF's professional incapacity were evident to close observers of South Vietnam's armed forces. At the center of that incapacity was a highly politicized and venal officer corps and a soldiery whose high desertion rates reflected at bottom an understandable unwillingness to die for "leaders" who cared only for themselves. Both President Ngo Dinh Diem and his military successors elevated political loyalty over professional competence as the key to promotion and other rewards. Key RVNAF units were withheld from combat to protect the government from the ever-present threat of a coup d'etat, and generals that displayed too much professional skill were always regarded as potential political threats. Additionally, military promotions and such important administrative offices as province chieftainships were more often than not offered to the highest politically acceptable bidder. An ambitious and politically acceptable colonel, for example, would pay to become a province chief, a position financed in turn by the sale of subordinate district chieftainships and the shakedown of local merchants.

There was also widespread theft of American military and economic aid. Stealing became obscenely profitable in a relatively small and poor country suddenly flooded with American wealth, and it was certainly easier and much safer than fighting the enemy, which, after all, the Americans in 1965 had volunteered to take care of anyway. Black market operations trafficking in U.S. goods stolen or bribed away from vast U.S. and RVN warehouses was a major feature of RVNAF corruption. There was nothing that could not be had for the right price on the teeming black market, including U.S. arms, ammunition, military radios, and medicine. Communist agents plied the market, especially for items, such as medicines, in short supply among Communist field forces. No wonder that the professional attractiveness of combat command that was paramount in other armies was notable for its absence in the RVNAF, where the lure of material gain was well-nigh irresistible. The National Military Academy in Dalat (South Vietnam's West Point) graduated officers that wanted staff rather than line billets; in one 1966 class, every graduating officer expressed preference for assignment to a division headquarters rather than an infantry company.[87]

A postwar survey of exiled South Vietnamese military officers and civilian leaders revealed that "corruption was considered more than a problem that could have been solved by the firing of a few generals or civilians. It was regarded by many of the respondents as a fundamental ill that was largely responsible for the ultimate collapse of South Vietnam."[88] Stewart Herrington argues that venality was so pervasive that purging the corrupt would have "decimated the officer corps . . . . To have attempted to cut out the cancer would have killed the patient."[89]

The ultimate corruption--and testimony to Vietnamization's innate futility--was spiritual: the RVNAF's unwillingness to seek battle with the Communists. Vietnamization armed and trained, but it could not create superior and combative leadership.[90] The RVNAF undoubtedly recognized the Communists' superior fighting power which, as Anthony James Joes correctly points out, stemmed in no small measure from (1) presentation of an attractive political program of "expel the foreigner, give the land to the peasants, and unite the nation," (2) a totalitarian political system that disciplined, controlled, and directed society far more effectively than possible in South Vietnam, and (3) a "military doctrine and fielded armed forces well-suited to both the aims and the territory for which they were fighting."[91] The RVNAF leadership also hoped, after 1965, and probably believed, that the Americans would win the war for them. However, even when it became apparent that the Americans were going to leave without having done so, the RVN, preoccupied with politics and rotted with corruption, proved incapable of endowing its officer corps or soldiery with the ingredients necessary to become competitive with the PAVN.

Lack of aggressiveness was reinforced by class antagonisms within the RVNAF. The rank and file was drawn from the peasantry, whereas the officer corps was recruited almost entirely from among the urban, educated, and socially advantaged strata of society. A greatly disproportionate number of senior officers were also Catholic--in a predominately Buddhist and animist country. (The legendary U.S. Army adviser John Paul Vann regarded these class and other differences separating the officer corps from the ranks as unbridgeable and, as such, a powerful argument for U.S. assumption of direct control of the RVNAF.[92]) The differences were all too often reflected in officer contempt for the common soldier (similar to the class arrogance and callousness that separated officer from enlisted man in the pre-1914 British army), to which the latter predictably responded with fear, distrust, and desertion. At no time during the Vietnam War did South Vietnam's senior leadership see fit to provide its troops even minimally adequate pay, dependent housing, medical care, and rotation out of isolated and vulnerable outpost duty. Open physical abuse of enlisted men and even junior officers for sins real and imagined was not uncommon.

The RVNAF's high desertion rates[93] came as no surprise, nor did the soldiers' propensity to supplement their meager pay through theft of foodstuffs from villages they entered by day but abandoned before dark. Unlike the Communist enemy it faced, the RVNAF lacked the two things that could have compensated for the perennial poverty, homesickness, and fear of death common to soldiers on both sides: superb discipline and a powerful and unifying patriotism capable of eliciting a willingness to sacrifice one's life on behalf of a larger cause. "The South Vietnamese soldier, in the end," concludes Guenter Lewy, "did not feel he was part of a political community worth the supreme sacrifice; he saw no reason to die for the [government]. The country lacked a political leadership which could inspire a sense of trust, purpose, and self-confidence."[94]

At bottom, the RVN was unsustainable because it failed to achieve the measure of political legitimacy necessary to compete with the Communists. William J. Duiker, the leading American historian of Vietnamese Communism, argues persuasively that the most important factor underlying the defeat of the RVN was the Communist Party's "successful effort to persuade millions of Vietnamese in both North and South that it was the sole legitimate representative of Vietnamese nationalism and national independence." This success was personified in the charismatic Ho Chi Minh, whose public personality, "embodying the qualities of virtue, integrity, dedication, and revolutionary asceticism, transcended issues of party and ideology and came to represent . . . the struggle for independence and self-realization of the Vietnamese nation."[95]

In Vietnam, anti-Communism was always burdened by its initial association with detested French rule (many senior RVNAF leaders had fought on the French side during the First Indochinese War) and by its antipathy to the powerful Vietnamese nationalist sentiment mobilized by Ho Chi Minh against both the French and their American successors. Additionally, as the Americans assumed ever greater responsibility for the anti-Communist struggle, the more they compromised the RVN's claim even to a pretense of national legitimacy. The situation became acute with the Americanization of the war beginning in 1965. The deployment of over half a million U.S. troops to South Vietnam, observes Timothy J. Lomperis,

> made it difficult for the Saigon government to hold on to its claims of traditional legitimacy, and correspondingly easy for

the Communists to depict themselves as champions against yet another foreign intervenor and to link themselves with all the heroes of the past who had fought against the intrusions of outsiders. If the Americans thought they were very different from Frenchmen, they did not appear to be to the villagers.[96]

The anti-Communist side was simply noncompetitive.

> What made the situation even worse was that the South Vietnamese leaders had very few claims of their own to national legitimacy. Although Ngo Dinh Diem was a nationalist, he did very little to show his sentiments during the struggle against the French. The subsequent leaders, Nguyen Cao Ky and Nguyen Van Thieu, both served in the French armed forces; thus, whatever sympathies they had for independence did not come into public view. Naturally, these facts and the presence of American troops redounded to the credit of the Communists. They also played a useful role in deflecting attention from the fundamental incompatibility between Marxism and the nature of traditional Vietnamese legitimacy. The Communists might not have gotten away with this if American troops had not been so conspicuously present.[97]

An inescapable conclusion is that the RVN, sponsored and sustained in the wake of what was intended to be a temporary division of Vietnam, was little more than an artifact of U.S. Cold War diplomacy, and in its short life failed to achieve the political legitimacy necessary to survive without a powerful U.S. military presence. "We are so powerful that Hanoi is simply unable to defeat us militarily. By its own efforts, Hanoi cannot force the withdrawal of American forces from South Vietnam," noted Henry Kissinger in 1969. "Unfortunately, our military strength has no political corollary; we have been unable . . . to create a political structure that could survive military opposition from Hanoi after we withdraw."[98] Concludes George C. Herring, the dean of American historians of the Vietnam War:

> Originally created by the French, the Saigon regime could never overcome its origins as a puppet government. Political fragmentation, the lack of able and farsighted leaders, and a tired and corrupt elite which could not adjust to the revolution that swept Vietnam after 1945 afforded a perilously weak basis

for nationhood. Given these harsh realities, the American effort to create a bastion of anticommunism south of the seventeenth parallel was probably doomed from the start.[99]

In Iraq, as in South Vietnam, political success will require creation of (1) a government regarded as legitimate by the great majority of the country's inhabitants, and (2) security forces capable of protecting the new political order. South Vietnam had a government, albeit a corrupt one, and large security forces, albeit professionally mediocre ones. Politically and militarily, however, it faced an exceptionally powerful enemy. In Iraq, the United States is starting from scratch because no real national government and only fledgling security forces exist. Moreover, any government the United States fosters in Iraq will be tainted in the eyes of many Iraqis by virtue of its American association, especially if the security situation continues to require a large and highly visible U.S. military presence. On the other hand, Sunni Arab alienation has failed to generate a political and military threat to state-building in Iraq remotely approaching that posed by the Communists in Vietnam. The main threat to state-building in Iraq lies not in the insurgency in central Iraq, but rather in the potential for the recent uprising of Shi'ite militants to reignite, expand, and include large elements of that community or the development of the kind of sectarian civil war that plunged Lebanon into near anarchy for almost 2 decades.

Prospects for creating a stable, prosperous, and democratic Iraq are problematic, and observers and decisionmakers should not be mislead by false analogies to American state-building success in Germany and Japan after World War II.[100] Among other things, the United States entered Germany and Japan with overwhelming force, precluding any postwar resistance; and in Japan, the Emperor Hirohito himself legitimized General Douglas MacArthur's military rule. The United States was also able to maintain an internationally supported military presence in Japan and Germany for years during which democratic institutions could be created and nurtured.

In Iraq, however, the United States does not have the luxury of time. Many Iraqis and virtually all of Iraq's Arab neighbors view the American military presence with profound suspicion; even those Iraqis who fear U.S. withdrawal will spark a civil war nonetheless distrust American motives in the region. Fueling pervasive anti-

Americanism in Iraq are regional media, especially Iranian and Gulf Arab state-based television programs. Iraqi governmental institutions are thus being hastily erected under extreme political pressure and have to be adapted and restructured in response to the objections of various Iraqi sectarian leaders, most notably Shi'ite Grand Ayatollah 'Ali Sistani.

That said, there is probably no feasible alternative to adherence to the June 30, 2004, deadline for transferring sovereignty to whatever Iraqi political entity finally is established to receive it. Many leading Iraqi politicians have deflected criticism of their cooperation with the United States by claiming that such cooperation is the best way to encourage an early U.S. military departure and pave the way for self-government. A significantly delayed departure--and certainly a perception of a permanent U.S. military presence in the making-- would threaten those politicians' credibility. Additionally, the more the United States attempts to bolster an indigenous government by a large and prolonged military presence, the more it is likely to undermine that government's legitimacy. Clear signs of a U.S. withdrawal will defuse nationalist concern and provide Iraqi governmental and especially security institutions some political breathing room.

The United States nonetheless is gambling regardless of what it does; if a prolonged military presence threatens to delegitimize the new Iraqi government, a premature and abrupt withdrawal could create a security vacuum encouraging disorder, even civil war.

Under even the best of circumstances, fashioning genuine democracy in post-Saddam Hussein Iraq is problematic. Since its creation, Iraq has known nothing but authoritarian rule and, under Saddam Hussein, a vicious neo-Stalinist tyranny. Though Iraqi regimes, like other dictatorships, embraced such democratic trappings as elections, parliaments, independent courts, they did so fraudulently for purely propaganda purposes. Thus for a democratic Iraq to work, Iraqis must accept the American claim that heretofore fraudulent institutions have been transformed into legitimate ones that can be trusted to deliver genuine representative government while protecting the rights of minorities.

Iraqis also are going to have to develop the kind of political society whereby contending individuals and groups can be elected to power without provoking fears of an existential threat among the losers. If the losers believe that the winners, once in office, will maintain power by extra-legal means, they may seek to ensure the safety of their own communities via resistance to national institutions and enhancing their own sources of power (such as militias). Democracy means different things to different communities in Iraq. To the majority Shi'ite Arabs, democracy is often viewed solely as a majority rule, winner-take-all system; anything less raises fear of a resurrected Sunni Arab tyranny and has incited the expressed concerns of Shi'ite leaders such as Grand Ayatollah Sistani. It is not clear that the Shi'ite leadership understands or accepts the concept of minority rights, rule of law, and other democratic principles unrelated to majority rule.

In Iraq, there are also questions about the current post-Saddam institutions that were created to ease the transition to democracy. The Iraq Governing Council (IGC) is a U.S.-appointed body containing a number of exiles who have little or no political standing inside Iraq and who, many Iraqis fear, can be manipulated by foreign interests. The IGC has also run afoul of the lower-level but more democratic councils selected with strong local support and legitimacy, portending future conflict between popular local councils and an unpopular national government. Additionally, the IGC and other Iraqi institutions have been called upon to function in a security environment dominated by the ever-present threat of assassination of themselves and their families.

Problems with the IGC, however, may soon be dwarfed by difficulties with a new government created under Iraq's controversial "Transitional Administrative Law" (TAL) or "interim Constitution" and the still unresolved efforts to create conditions under which elections can be held in Iraq.[101] The TAL emerged only after fierce disagreement and continues to enjoy only the most conditional support by those Iraqis who tolerate it at all.[102] Key issues addressed by the TAL but still subject to dispute include the structure of government, the role of Islam in public life, Kurdish autonomy, and the nature of federalism.

Under the TAL, executive power is to be concentrated in a three-person executive council composed of a president and two deputy presidents. The president is widely expected to be a Shi'ite Arab, with a Sunni Arab and a Kurd serving as deputy presidents. All three executives must agree on any policy initiative before it is undertaken. The unanimity rule offers the minority Sunni and Kurdish communities some protection, but Shi'ite leaders are livid about a system of governance which they believe cheats them of their rightful (majoritarian) leadership of the country. Additionally, much to the anger of the Shi'ites, the TAL grants three predominantly Kurdish provinces the right to reject a future permanent Constitution. According to the Grand Ayatollah Sistani, the most respected Shi'ite leader in the country, "This constitution that gives the presidency in Iraq to a three-member council, a Kurd, a Sunni Arab, and a Shi'ite Arab, enshrines sectarianism and ethnicity in the future political system in the country."[103] Sistani has warned UN officials that he will refrain from working with them should they do anything to bolster the legitimacy of the interim Constitution.[104]

Disagreements over election-related issues also have been serious. Initial U.S. plans for regional caucuses (involving indirect elections) to produce a transitional government were strongly opposed by the Shi'ite religious leadership, including Sistani, and consequently had to be cancelled. An alternative to caucuses has yet to be developed, but the Shi'tes have made it very clear that they will not accept any solution, including indirect elections and weighted voting, other than "one person, one vote."

The Kurds, however, are unlikely to accept the Shi'ite demand for absolute majority rule because historically they were victimized by a strong central government in Baghdad and because they have enjoyed virtual political autonomy since the end of the Gulf War 1991. Accordingly, the Kurds favor a weak, even paralyzed, central government; they seek to preserve as much of their post-1991 autonomy as they can, as well as to claim as much of Iraq's oil resources and revenues as they can for their own region. The Kurds remain thoroughly alienated from the Iraqi state and have a powerful sense of nationhood.[105] Many young Kurds no longer even learn Arabic in the schools in the Kurdish autonomous areas.

Sunni Arabs are likewise concerned about a new power sharing arrangement based on majority rule. In the aftermath of the U.S. de-Ba'athification campaign, Sunnis are widely reported to feel a strong sense of uncertainty, fear, and persecution. Some assert that de-Ba'athification aims to prepare the country for a Shi'ite leadership dependent on the United States.[106] Many Sunnis are certain that the United States has given up on them and is conspiring with the

Shi'ite Arabs to do them in politically, a view that manifestly fuels insurgent violence against U.S. forces.

Ironically, the development of democratic institutions in Iraq is likely to stimulate formation of political parties based on ethic and sectarian allegiances that would simply magnify the sharp divisions within Iraqi society. As experience in other developing countries shows, sectarian political parties seldom have a stake in political moderation because they appeal for support within the same ethnic group by articulating the demands of their community at the expense of seeking broad support on a transcommunal basis. In so doing, they often attempt to outbid each other in their assertiveness in claiming a larger share of political power for their own group. In such an environment, compromising leaders can be tarred as "sellouts" and the election of a radical party from one sectarian community can provoke the rise of radical leadership in other communities, thus sparking a cycle virtually guaranteed to produce violent intercommunal confrontation and the disintegration of any pretense of democracy.[107]

Even assuming success in the creation of a stable government commanding the loyalty or at least the passive acquiescence of most Iraqis, the new state will still need army and security forces capable protecting it from internal and external threats. It is certainly in the interest of the United States as well as any new Iraqi government to transfer military and police functions now being shouldered by the United States as quickly as feasible to indigenous institutions. As Secretary of Defense Donald Rumsfeld has stated, referring to U.S. and coalition forces in Iraq, "foreign forces are unnatural. They ought not to be in a country."[108] The "Iraqization" of security functions now being performed by U.S. forces and the concomitant withdrawal of those forces are likely to bolster the legitimacy of any new Iraq government, provided that the new forces can operate without extensive and visible support from U.S. troops remaining in the country after the turnover of sovereignty to Iraqis scheduled for June 30, 2004. The United States plans to organize, train, and equip over 200,000 Iraqi security personnel as part of this effort.[109]

But those forces must be effective. The CPA's mid-May 2003 decision, for reasons not well-explained, to disband the entire Iraqi regular army with but a month's pay is now widely regarded as a mistake. According to one source:

> The dismissal of [Iraqi officers] treated them as an extension of Saddam and the Ba'ath's rule . . . rather than as patriots who had fought for their country. It also added several hundred thousand men to the labor pool when there were virtually no jobs, and it effectively told all officers of the rank of colonel and above that they had no future in a post-Saddam environment. At the same time, it implied to all Iraqis that the new Iraq Army might be so weak that Iraq would remain little more than a client of the United States and Britain in the face of the threat from Iran and possible future intervention by Turkey.[110]

The decision was not reversed, nor have selective recalls been implemented; instead, the New Iraqi Army (NIA) is being created from scratch. The New Iraqi Army is the third name given to the force. The first was the "New Iraqi Corps," but the acronym for this sounds like an Arab expletive. "Iraqi Defense Forces" was then tried but discarded because its acronym is identical to that of the Israeli Defense Forces.

Though the primary mission of the NIA is protection of Iraq from external attack, as opposed to providing internal security, this mission seems to have been set aside, at least temporarily, because of urgent counterinsurgency requirements in the so-called Sunni triangle area. Indeed, some NIA troops were placed in the most dangerous Sunni areas shortly after they completed their training.[111]

Early planning behind the NIA rested on the apparent assumption that Iraq could initially satisfy its security needs with a small, 40,000-man army composed primarily of light infantry (compared to the 350,000-man heavy-and-light army that Iraq had at the beginning of the war.)[112] The NIA was to be created over a 3-year period, although this schedule was subsequently reduced to 2 years because of the ongoing lack of security in central Iraq. The new schedule calls for an NIA of 12,000 by July 2004 and the full 40,000 by mid-2005.[113] A larger NIA is also being considered. However, the first NIA battalion crumbled when up to one-half of its members deserted because of inadequate pay and risky combat assignments in the Sunni Triangle; some said they could make better money by cooperating with the insurgents in killing U.S. troops.[114] Pay was subsequently raised and conditions were improved.

Two other major problems with the NIA have caused yet additional disincentives to join it: insurgent attacks on recruiting stations, and the NIA's lack of all but small arms. The latter, especially given the insurgency's near monopoly of the tactical initiative vis-à-vis the NIA, places the NIA at a considerable combat disadvantage.

Police units are another especially important element in the effort to create and maintain security because their primary mission is internal security. Not surprisingly, police force units have attracted repeated insurgent attacks, and there are reports that the police may have been infiltrated by some insurgent elements.[115] By April 2004, at least 350 Iraqi police officers had been killed in confrontations with insurgents.[116] One estimate even suggested that the number was 632.[117] Moreover, in a disturbing April 2004 development, a number of Iraqi police units abandoned their posts rather than resist poorly-trained militiamen loyal to Muqtada al Sadr.[118]

In addition to the NIA and the police, new Iraqi security forces include the Iraqi Border Guard (IBG), Iraqi facility protection units, and the Iraqi Civil Defense Corps (ICDC). The ICDC is the most important of these three forces because its mission is counterinsurgency, which it is expected to perform without the presence of coalition forces.

The ICDC, whose necessity, like the insurgency itself, was not anticipated before the war, was created in July 2003 in response to the insurgency and began operations in August.[119] Efforts to organize, train, and equip the ICDC, originally designed as a temporary force (to be disbanded once the insurgency ended), lagged behind those of the NIA and police. As expected with any new Iraqi force, the ICDC has a mixed record and depends heavily on U.S. advice, training, and money, though it is considered an emerging success by CENTCOM and Defense Department officials.[120]

The Iraq Civil Defense Corps has some clear advantages within Iraqi society. Many of its members strongly and credibly claim they are fighting for the protection of their local community and are not supporters of either the coalition presence or the U.S.-supported Iraqi government.[121] Moreover, in many areas, especially in small towns and rural places, Iraqis have joined the ICDC with the approval and support of the local tribal leadership, thus legitimizing their membership in the ICDC as well as their performance of its counter-insurgent mission. Finally, as a local defense force, the ICDC, whose units take only 3 weeks to train, has advantages in gathering intelligence.

How the Iraqi security forces stand in the eyes of the citizens they are charged with protecting is not clear, although anecdotal information suggests that they are dimly viewed by some clergy and many Sunni Arabs. It is in any event difficult to build new security forces accepted as legitimate in the absence of an actual Iraqi government regarded as such. And Iraqi security forces well may wonder what will happen to them when U.S. forces depart. In a worrisome potential precedent, some ICDC units deserted their posts during the Muqtada al Sadr uprising.[122]

The alternatives to U.S.-sponsored security institutions in Iraq are communal militias. If Iraqis come to lack confidence in the NIA and ICDC, they will look to such militias for protection. Though the United States rightly regards Iraq's "militia-ization" as a recipe for civil war, and has sought to demobilize existing militias and thwart the formation of new ones, armed Iraqi communities have little incentive to strip themselves of means of protection. Various groups are reportedly stockpiling and hiding weapons even as they publicly claim to be moving toward demobilization. Moreover, many political groups are seeking to place as many of their own members as possible in the new Iraqi security institutions. Should sectarian strife erupt, these institutions will likely dissolve into armed factions, and given Iraq's strong sectarianism and as yet weak élan of the new Iraqi security institutions, loyalty to one's community almost certainly will trump fidelity to those institutions.[123]

Domestic Political Sustainability.

The American war effort in Vietnam failed because it became unsustainable at home. Though the United States was militarily unbeatable in Vietnam, it lacked the political stakes in the war that the Communists had. In the end, the Vietnam War boiled down to a contest of political wills, and the Communists had the stronger. Secretary of State Dean Rusk acknowledged after the war that "I made two mistakes with respect to Vietnam. First, I overestimated the patience of the American people, and second, I underestimated the tenacity of the North Vietnamese."[124] General Vo Nguyen Giap, who led Communist forces against the French and later became North Vietnam's minister of defense, told journalist Stanley Karnow in 1990 that

We were not strong enough to drive out a half-million American troops, but that wasn't our aim. Our intention was to break the will of the American Government to continue the war. Westmoreland was wrong to expect that his superior firepower would grind us down. If we had [attempted to pit our material inferiority directly against your superiority], we would have been defeated in 2 hours.[125]

The turning point was the Tet Offensive, a military defeat for the Communists but a political shock for the United States. Tet, for all to see, popped the balloon of official optimism on the war. For the preceding half-year, Johnson administration spokesmen, in a White House orchestrated campaign, declared that the corner had been turned in Vietnam, that the Communists were in permanent retreat, and that the end of the war was in sight. The size and savagery of the Communist assault, which inflicted the highest weekly and monthly U.S. manpower loss rates of the war, belied these claims and suggested the prospect of an endless military stalemate, of more and more American bloodshed without convincing progress toward the declared U.S. objective of a Communist-free South Vietnam.[126]

Large public and congressional majorities, as well as editorial opinion of such mainstream liberal newspapers as the *Washington Post* and *New York Times*, supported U.S. military intervention in the Vietnam War, and support for staying the course in Vietnam remained strong, notwithstanding rising casualties and a growing domestic anti-war movement, as long as the United States seemed, however slowly, to be winning the war in a reasonable amount of time.[127] Underlying this support were high levels of trust in the competence and integrity of the U.S. Government, especially on matters of war and peace, a trust that diminished as the war continued, and opposition to the war within America's opinion-making elite increased. By March 1969, a year after the Tet Offensive and 4 years after the deployment of U.S. ground combat forces to Vietnam, U.S. battle deaths equaled those of the highly unpopular 3-year Korean War, and nearly two out of three Americans polled said they would have opposed U.S. entry into the Vietnam War had they known what it would cost in American lives.[128]

Studies of the Vietnam and other American wars of the 20th century reveal that, contrary to the post-Vietnam War conventional wisdom that profound casualty aversion dominates all other considerations in determining war and peace decisions, most Americans are influenced by such pragmatic considerations as the perceived stakes at hand and benefits of intervention, chances of success, possible and actual costs, alterations in initial and subsequent expectations, and elite opinion.[129] U.S. political and military leaders may have convinced themselves that the American public is intolerant of casualties;[130] in fact, however, "support for U.S. military operations and the willingness to tolerate casualties are based upon a sensible weighing of benefits and costs that is influenced heavily by consensus (or its absence) among political leaders."[131] Writing on the matter of casualties 2 decades after the fall of Saigon but with the Vietnam War clearly in mind, Richard K. Betts observed:

> There is no clear evidence that Americans will not tolerate many body bags in the course of intervention where vital interests are not at stake. What is crucial for maintaining public support is not casualties per se, but casualties in an *inconclusive* war, casualties that the public sees as being suffered indefinitely, for no clear, good, or achievable purpose.[132]

This was certainly the situation that confronted the Nixon administration when it took office in 1969, and accounts in large measure for the administration's decision to eliminate conscription and to launch a unilateral, incremental withdrawal of U.S. forces from that country absent any political concessions from the Communists.[133] From April 1969 to December 1972, U.S. military personnel in Vietnam dropped from 543,000 to 24,000, with battle dead during the same years falling from 9,377 to 300.[134] The strength of the domestic political imperative was evident in Nixon's determination to proceed with a unilateral pullout even though he clearly understood that a shrinking U.S. force presence reduced his bargaining leverage with the Communists.

In Iraq by mid-April 2004, U.S. military dead (due to hostile action and accidents) totaled 685, with over 3,000 additional American troops wounded. Most of these casualties were incurred after President Bush declared the termination of major combat operations on May 1, 2003; that phase of the war cost the United States only 138 dead and 550 wounded.[135] After May 1, 2003, casualties fluctuated from month to month, rising to 82 dead in November then dropping to 22 dead in February 2004, then rising again to 92 dead in just the first half of April. Future losses are unpredictable. Much will depend on the general security situation in Iraq, U.S. military adaptability to changing enemy tactics, and the degree to which expanding Iraqi security forces can and will assume functions currently performed by U.S. military forces. The planned transfer of sovereignty to Iraqis on June 30, 2004, is intended to reduce U.S. loss rates, although this increasingly appears unlikely.

Additionally, American casualties incurred in Iraq may have less domestic political salience than those of the Vietnam War, which was waged largely by conscripts and draft-induced "volunteers." Though the inequitable draft system enabled most college students to avoid military service, many opponents of the war, including collegiate protestors, were politicized by fear of and anger over conscription. Today, without conscription, fewer Americans feel their lives and futures are directly threatened by the conflict in Iraq than was the case during the Vietnam War. The situation may make the conflict more sustainable to the general public by removing an important personal element from the calculation of nonvolunteers and their families and friends, although it threatens to reduce the number of volunteers should the war become bloodier.

Yet even reduced casualties may not guarantee sustainability in Iraq. In the Vietnam War, casualties were not the only war cost that undermined public support. Other costs included increased taxes, inflation, diminished investment in popular domestic programs, rising elite dissensus over the war, political turmoil at home, disdain for South Vietnam as a worthy ally, and a growing "credibility gap" between official and unofficial portrayals of what was going on in Vietnam. However, as a 1985 Rand Corporation study pointed out, casualties "are the most visible and least tolerable cost imposed by direct U.S. combat involvement in sustained limited wars. Mounting casualties tend over time to undermine public support for limited wars, and in addition serve as a lightning rod for public dissatisfaction with other issues."[136] Robert Komer, who directed the pacification program in Vietnam, told a Rand Corporation interviewer after the war that:

> The most obvious and immediate cost is the cost of casualties. The death notices in the newspapers and so forth. Remember what it costs you in blood is much more politically visible than what it costs you in treasures . . . . Casualties become a problem because they are cumulative. You spend a lot of money, but then you have another appropriation the following fiscal and the year after that. But casualties mount up, and they have a psychological and political impact over time.[137]

Other studies support casualties as the primary barometer of American public support (or lack of support) for limited wars, which are often prolonged and waged in faraway places, with military restraint, and on behalf of abstract objectives.[138] It is widely believed that democracies in general have great difficulty prosecuting protracted wars for limited objectives. Such wars are, as was Vietnam, wars of choice rather than wars of necessity, which engage existential interests. Vietnam certainly deviated from the preferred American way of war. Americans have not been comfortable with limited wars because they tend to separate war and politics, believing that war is a substitute for, rather than an extension of, politics. Once the shooting begins, and regardless of political objective, so the thinking goes, the aim should be the enemy's total military defeat. The "unconditional surrender" formula of Ulysses S. Grant and Franklin D. Roosevelt has been the ideal, not the compromise Korean War armistice or the hesitant gradualism that many still believe led to America's defeat in Vietnam.[139]

The question of whether the Iraq War of 2003 was a war of necessity is one of several key factors bearing on the political sustainability of the ongoing U.S. effort to create a stable, prosperous, and democratic Iraq. Another key factor will be Americans' judgments on the war's ongoing costs as weighed against perceived gains. If the Iraq War comes to be seen as a war of choice rather than a war of necessity, then its costs may require compensation by some additional measure of national security gain, such as the as yet unrealized and increasingly unlikely recession of Arab radicalism and a wider acceptance of the United States in the Middle East.

In the absence of national security gains, Americans may feel comforted by such humanitarian gains as the overthrow of Saddam Hussein's monstrous regime. But Americans could become very impatient should the rationale for a continuing and costly U.S.

occupation of Iraq shift to a more direct focus on uplifting the Iraqi people, especially if the Iraq public appears ungrateful and turns hostile.

To date, there is no evidence that U.S. casualty rates in Iraq, which are a fraction of those incurred in Vietnam, have generated sufficient public sentiment to evacuate Iraq or even reduce U.S. objectives in that country. Nor, unlike the Vietnam War, has the Iraq War and its aftermath caused inflation and prompted increased taxes; on the contrary, inflation has been minimal and tax relief has been the order of the day. Nor has there been any disruptive antiwar turmoil in the streets (which during the Vietnam War was fueled in part by conscription) or effective congressional check on administration Iraq policy.

On the other hand, public and congressional tolerance for casualties may have dropped by virtue of failure to find any WMD in Iraq or to uncover any convincing evidence of a prewar operational relationship between Iraq and al-Qaeda, to say nothing of Iraqi complicity in the 9/11 attacks. Moreover, U.S. taxpayer costs in Iraq, together with tax cuts and other factors, are contributing to unprecedented annual federal deficits and a cumulative national debt that could have perilous economic consequences in the long run.

Prewar portrayals of a "grave and gathering" threat posed by Saddam Hussein to the United States and its overseas interests convinced many that preventive war against Iraq was a necessity--and therefore worth considerable risk and loss. But the postwar deflation of that portrayal suggests that Operation IRAQI FREEDOM was a war of choice and as such, like Vietnam, a war bounded by significant limits on public tolerance of risk and loss. Reinforcing these limits are the unexpected difficulties and costs the United States has encountered in Iraq since the President declared the termination of major combat operations in that country. Prewar assertions that U.S. forces would be universally welcomed as liberators inside Iraq, that U.S. occupation authorities would inherit functioning government infrastructure capable of providing essential government services pending the restoration of sovereignty, and that Iraq's restored oil revenues would finance its economic reconstruction all foundered on the rocks of Iraqi insurgent attacks on U.S. forces and reconstruction targets, Iraq's administrative disintegration, and the discovery that

Iraq's oil, power, and water infrastructure was crippled far beyond expectation.[140]

Yet the long-term effect on public opinion of these disparities between expectations and realities remains to be seen. The U.S. death toll in Iraq is low by the standards of past major wars, and most Americans in a presidential election year are preoccupied with other matters. A mid-December 2003 CNN/*USA Today*/Gallup poll revealed that 61 percent of Americans polled believed that the situation in Iraq was worth going to war for (v. a negative response of 35 percent), and that 53 percent believed Saddam was personally involved of the September 11, 2001 terrorist attacks on the United States (v. 42 percent). Sixty-five percent of those polled expressed approval of the way the United States was handling the situation in Iraq since the termination of major U.S. combat operations there (v. 34 percent).[141] These numbers suggest that most Americans at the end of 2003 still regarded the Iraq War as a war of necessity and so far worth the cost in blood and treasure.

Polls taken in the first three months of 2004, however, registered a significant decline in public support. A CNN/*USA Today*/Gallup poll taken January 29 to February 1 revealed that only 49 percent of those polled believed that it "was worth going to war in Iraq," and that 43 percent believed that the "administration deliberately misled the American public about whether Iraq [had] weapons of mass destruction." The same poll also found that only 46 percent approved of the way the administration "is handling the situation in Iraq."[142] This decline in public support was confirmed in two subsequent March polls by the *Washington Post*-ABC News and the *Wall Street Journal*-NBC News.[143] A Gallup Poll taken in early April revealed that only 50 percent of the American public believed that it was "worth going to war" in Iraq (47 percent said it was not worth going to war), and that 64 percent believed that things were "going moderately badly, or very badly" in Iraq (only 34 percent believed things were going "very well or moderately well.")[144]

As of mid-April 2004, the scope and costs of the U.S. counterinsurgency war in Iraq appeared politically sustainable, until problems in the Shi'ite areas raised new questions about the possibility of a wider war. The Iraqi insurgency, at this point, nevertheless bears no comparison in terms of size, ideological appeal, and political base to the Communist challenge we faced in Vietnam.

This could change, however, if the insurgency were to expand in a sustained and meaningful way to Iraq's majority Shi'ites or if the Iraqi state were violently to disintegrate into its constituent sectarian parts. In either of these circumstances--a national liberation war against a detested occupier or Iraq's "Lebanonization"--it would be extremely difficult for the United States to maintain its military position, to say nothing of its political objectives, in that country.

A major determinant of the course of events in Iraq will be Iraqi responses to the U.S. transfer of sovereignty to an as yet undetermined Iraqi political entity, scheduled for June 30. Will that entity command sufficient legitimacy and security forces to lead Iraq into stable and popular governance, or will it prove too weak to survive the eruption of centrifugal political forces inside Iraq?

CONCLUSIONS AND RECOMMENDATIONS

1. Though policymakers instinctively turn to what they think history teaches about what to do, or not do, in a given foreign policy situation, reasoning by historical analogy is an inherently risky business. No two historical situations are identical, and policymakers' knowledge of history is often poor. Policymakers are, in any event, predisposed to embrace analogies, however faulty, that support preferred policy.[143] Thus proponents of the Iraq War embraced the Munich analogy (and the success of U.S. state-building in Japan and Germany), whereas opponents of war warned of another Vietnam. Operation IRAQI FREEDOM achieved the "Munich" objective of eliminating a regime that proponents believed posed a gathering threat to the United States. Yet satisfaction of that objective simply confronted the United States with the unexpectedly costly and difficult challenges of state-building in circumstances of ongoing insurgent violence that some were prepared to label a Vietnam-like quagmire.

2. The decision to invade Iraq in 2003 and overthrow the Saddam Hussein regime cannot be repealed. As in Vietnam in 1965, U.S. power and prestige have been massively committed in Iraq, and it is incumbent upon the United States try its best to leave behind in Iraq a "better peace" than it found there, even if that means reconsidering some ambitious U.S. objectives in Iraq. What if, for example, the United States is forced to choose between stability and democracy in that volatile country? Many experts believe that genuine democracy lies beyond the power and patience of the United States to create in Iraq. If so, both Americans and Iraqis might have to settle for some form of benign quasi-authoritarian rule along the lines of Kemal Ataturk's Turkey, Anwar Sadat's Egypt, and King Hussein's Jordan, perhaps as a prolonged transition to more representative governance. However, under no circumstances--other than the descent of Iraq into uncontrollable civil war--should the United States abandon Iraq as it did South Vietnam in 1975. Indeed, abandonment would seem a near-guarantee of civil war, which could be a worse state of affairs for the average Iraqi than even the Stalinist tyranny of Saddam Hussein.[146]

3. *Policymakers must recognize that the differences between Iraq and Vietnam greatly outweigh the similarities, especially in the military dimensions of the two conflicts.* That said, it would be a mistake to underestimate Iraqi insurgents as the United States did the Vietnamese Communists in Indochina. After all, the very appearance of an insurgency after the termination of major U.S. combat operations surprised many. Moreover, though the nature, size, and appeal of the Iraqi insurgency bears no comparison to its Vietnamese Communist counterpart (except in so far as both insurgencies are expressions of irregular warfare), the Iraqi insurgency has so far and with increasing skill attacked targets that are key to Iraq's successful reconstruction. Dismissing the insurgents as "terrorists" and "dead-enders" overlooks the potentially dangerous downstream political consequences of establishing a large American force presence in an Arab heartland and attempting to transform Iraq into a pro-Western democracy. It was not expected that the minority Sunni Arab community would welcome a post-Saddam Iraq in which it no longer enjoyed a monopoly of power; but neither was it expected that U.S. postwar policies in Iraq would alienate many Shi'ites--some of them to the point of armed resistance, raising the prospect of a two-front insurgency.

4. *Policymakers must also recognize and understand the two most instructive dimensions of the Vietnam analogy for the current situation in Iraq: the challenges of state-building, and the need to maintain sufficient domestic political support.* On these two matters, the lessons of Vietnam need to be studied. State-building in Iraq could fail for the same principal reason it failed in South Vietnam: inability to create a

political order commanding popular legitimacy. Nor should open-ended domestic political support be taken for granted. The late President Richard Nixon once remarked: "When a president sends American troops off to war, a hidden timer starts to run. He has a finite period of time to win the war before the people grow weary of it."[147] As of this writing, the U.S. forces have just entered their second year in Iraq. If one were to follow the Vietnam War analogy, U.S. forces are in the spring of 1966--still 2 years away from the Tet Offensive, and almost 7 years away from the final U.S. military withdrawal from the conflict. However, the decisionmakers of 1965 could take for granted more sustainable levels of public support precisely because they did not, in contrast to the decisionmakers of 2003, have the cautionary experience of the Vietnam War behind them.

5. *Policymakers also should not take for granted the absence of hostile external state intervention in Iraq.* The absence of a North Vietnam analog in Iraq could change, depending on the course of events. For example, Iran, which has strong state and theocratic interests in Iraq that have so far been well-served by the U.S. destruction of the Saddam Hussein regime and the subsequent disorder in Iraq that has tied down U.S. ground forces that might otherwise have been available to threaten regime change in Teheran, is well-positioned to sponsor accelerated chaos in Iraq.[148] Iran has no interest in the resurrection of a powerful Iraq, and certainly not a democratic, pro-Western Iraq, and it has enough Revolutionary Guards and intelligence operatives to "get tens of thousands of Iraqi Shiites on the streets to protest the U.S. occupation."[149]

AFTERWORD

In closing this analysis, it is important to recognize perhaps the most important difference between the Vietnam War and the current conflict in Iraq: the former is a finished event, whereas the latter is an event in progress. We know what happened to Vietnam and U.S. policy there in the 1960s and 1970s; in contrast, the ultimate fate of Iraq and U.S. policy objectives in that country remains to be seen. Accordingly, some judgments on the differences and similarities between Iraq and Vietnam are necessarily tentative and could change as events unfold. This analysis is a snapshot of the apparent differences and similarities between Iraq and Vietnam taken in the spring of 2004.

ENDNOTES

1. Commentary on the Iraq War and its aftermath bulges with favorable and unfavorable references to the Vietnam War analogy. See, for example, Robert L. Bartley, "Iraq: Another Vietnam?" *Wall Street Journal*, November 3, 2003; Elizabeth Becker, "In the Ranks, Similarities Between Vietnam and Iraq," *New York Times*, November 2, 2003; Max Boot, "Forget Vietnam—History Deflates Guerrilla Mystique," *Los Angeles Times*, April 6, 2003; Robert J. Caldwell, "Iraq is No Vietnam," *San Diego Union-Tribune*, November 9, 2003; Hank Cole, "Iraq War Bears Resemblance to U.S. Efforts in Vietnam," *Colorado Springs Gazette*, December 9, 2003; "Facts Fail to Support Iraq-Vietnam Comparisons," *USA Today*, November 7, 2003; Howard Fineman, "Echoes of Vietnam Grow Louder," *Newsweek*, October 29, 2003; David Gelernter, "Don't Quit as We Did in Vietnam," *Los Angeles* Times, November 9, 2003; David Gergen, "The Fierce Urgency of Iraq," *U.S. News and World Report*, October 13, 2003; Bradley Graham, "Is Iraq Another Vietnam Quagmire? No and Yes," *Washington Post*, October 5, 2003; Richard Haloran, "Vietnam Syndrome Resurfaces in Iraq," *Honolulu Advertiser*, February 15, 2004; Victor Davis Hanson, "Then and Now," *National Review*, December 8, 2003; Seymour M. Hersh, "Moving Targets," *New Yorker*, December 15, 2003; John Hughes, "Why Iraq is Not Like Vietnam," *Christian Science Monitor*, August 27, 2003; Michael Ignatieff, "The American Empire (Get Used to It)," *New York Times Magazine*, January 5, 2003; Robert G. Kaiser, "Iraq Isn't Vietnam, But They Rhyme," *Washington Post*, December 28, 2003; James Kitfield, "No, It's Not Vietnam," *National Journal*, November 22, 2003; Stanley Karnow, "Do Not Compare Iraq with Vietnam," *Boston Globe*, April 20, 2003; Richard Leiby, "Iraq Vs. Vietnam: The Scorecard," *Washington Post*, March 21, 2004; Gordon Livingston, "Iraq's Chilling Echoes of Vietnam," *San Francisco Chronicle*, November 30, 2003; Sandra Mackey, *The Reckoning: Iraq and the Legacy of Saddam Hussein*, New York: W. W. Norton, 2002, p. 396; John Maggs, "Too Much Like Vietnam," *National Journal*, November 22, 2003; Michael Mandelbaum, "Iraq Doesn't Fit Vietnam Picture," *Long Island Newsday*, October 31, 2003; Dave Moniz, "Monthly Costs of Iraq, Afghan Wars Approach that of Vietnam," *USA Today*, September 8, 2003; Dave Moniz, "Some Veterans of Vietnam See Iraq Parallel in Lack of Candor," *USA Today*, November 7, 2003; Walter Pincus, "A Quagmire? More Like a Presidential Fixation," *Washington Post*, August 31, 2003; James P. Pinkerton, "Bush's War Strategy Looks Like a Steal of Nixon," *Long Island Newsday*, November 18, 2003; Thomas E. Ricks, "For Vietnam Vet Anthony Zinni, Another War on Shaky Territory," *Washington Post*, December 23, 2003; Thomas E. Ricks, "Marines to offer New Tactics in Iraq," *Washington Post*, January 7, 2004; Sally Satel, "Returning from Iraq, Still Fighting Vietnam," *New York* Times, March 5, 2004; Evan Thomas, Rod Nordlinger, and Christian Caryl,

"Operation Hearts and Minds," *Newsweek*, December 29, 2003-January 5, 2004; Mike Turner, "The Only Way Out is Forward," *Newsweek*, September 12, 2003; Craig R. Whitney, "Tunnel Vision: Watching Iraq, and Seeing Vietnam," *New York Times*, November 9, 2003; George C. Wilson, "Beware a Phoenix Rising from Iraq's Ashes," *National Journal*, December 20, 2003; and George C. Wilson, "Iraq in Not Vietnam," *National Journal*, April 12, 2003.

2. Harry G. Summers, Jr., *Vietnam War Almanac*, New York: Facts on File Publications, 1985, p. 113.

3. See John W, Garver, "The Chinese Threat and the Vietnam War," *Parameters*, Spring 1992, pp. 73-85.

4. Stephen Biddle, *et al.*, "Iraq and the Future of Warfare," Testimony Before the House Armed Services Committee in Operation IRAQI FREEDOM: An Outside Perspective, Hearings Before the Committee on Armed Services, U.S. House of Representatives, One Hundred Eighth Congress, First Session, October 2003.

5. Quoted in Larry Berman, *Planning a Tragedy: The Americanization of the War in Vietnam*, New York: W. W. Norton, 1982, p. 92.

6. The 35-year struggle for an independent, unified, and Communist Vietnam began with the 1946-54 French-Indochinese War and ended with the fall of South Vietnam in 1975. In 1955 the United States displaced the French in South Vietnam and 10 years later began major combat operations in Indochina which were terminated in 1973.

7. Shelby Stanton, *Vietnam Order of Battle*, Washington, DC: U.S. News Books, 1981, p. 333; David L. Anderson, *The Columbia Guide to the Vietnam War*, New York: Columbia University Press, 2002, pp. 286, 287, 288.

8. Spencer C. Tucker, ed., *Encyclopedia of the Vietnam War: A Political, Social, and Military History*, New York: Oxford University Press, 1998, p. 453; *Victory in Vietnam: The Official History of the People's Army of Vietnam, 1954-1975*, Merle L. Pribbenow, trans., Lawrence, KS: University of Kansas Press, 2002, p. 431.

9. See *Victory in Vietnam, op. cit.*, p. 211; James W. McCoy, *Secrets of the Viet Cong*, New York: Hippocrene Books, 1992, pp. 360-361; James J. Wirtz, *The Tet Offensive: Intelligence Failure and War*, Ithaca, NY: Cornell University Press, 1991, pp. 247-251; Phillip B. Davidson, *Vietnam at War: The History 1946-1975*, Novato, CA: Presidio Press, 1988, p. 475; and Tucker, *op. cit.*, p. 396.

10. "Live Video Teleconference with General Abizaid," *U.S. Department of Defense News Transcript*, November 13, 2003, *www.dod.mil.transcripts*.

11. Phillip S. Meilinger, *Air Power: Myths and Facts*, Maxwell AFB, AL; Air University Press, December 2003, p. 78.

12. Earl H. Tilford, Jr., *Crosswinds: The Air Force's Setup in Vietnam*, College Station, TX: Texas A&M University Press, 1993, p. xv; Mark Clodfelter, *The Limits of Air Power: The American Bombing of North Vietnam*, New York: Free Press, 1989, p. 8.

13. Anderson, *op. cit.*, p. 201.

14. Jeffrey Record, *The Wrong War: Why We Lost in Vietnam*, Annapolis, MD: Naval Institute Press, 1998, p. 119. For greater detail on helicopter and fixed-wing aircraft operations and losses, see Tucker, *op. cit.*, pp. 165-169; Raphael Littaeur and Norman Uphoff, eds., *The Air War in Indochina*, Revised ed., Boston: Beacon Press, 1972.

15. Anthony H. Cordesman, *The Iraq War: Strategy, Tactics, and Military Lessons*, Washington, DC: Center for Strategic and International Studies, 2002, p. 318.

16. "U.S. Helicopter Down in Iraq," BBC News Online, January 23, 2004; David A Fulghum, "SAMS Threaten," *Aviation Week and Space Technology*, February 2, 2004, p. 43.

17. Fulghum, *op. cit.*, p. 43.

18. Figures calculated from data appearing in Summers, *op. cit.*, p. 113; Anderson, *op. cit.*, p. 290. Dead include nonbattle deaths from accidents and other causes.

19. Figures include battle and nonbattle deaths, and for all but the Iraq War are calculated from casualty data appearing in Michael Clodfelter, *Warfare and Armed Conflicts: A Statistical Reference to Casualty and Other Figures, 1500-2000*, Second ed., Jefferson, NC: McFarland and Company, Inc., 2002, pp. 481, 584, 659, and 735. The daily dead number for the Gulf War includes nonbattle deaths (151) incurred during Operation DESERT SHIELD.

20. Cordesman, *op. cit.*, p. 238.

21. Reuters, "U.S. Toll in Iraq at 645," *Los Angeles Times*, April 9, 2004, internet and Associated Press, "A Look at U.S. Military Deaths in Iraq," *New York Times* on the Web, March 22, 2004; and Tom quitieri, "Rumsford Says Recent Losses Not Forseen," *USA Today*, April 16, 2004.

22. Americans, including the U.S. military, have a tendency to explain the success or failure of American arms on the basis of what the United States did or did not do. This narcissism often undervalues what the enemy did or did not do.

23. See Andrew Mack, "Why Big Nations Lose Small Wars: The Politics of Asymmetric Conflict," *World Politics*, Vol. 27, 1975, pp. 176-220.

24. Fighting power consists of "the moral, intellectual, and organizational dimensions" of military power as manifested is such things as "discipline and cohesion, morale and initiative, courage and toughness, the willingness to fight and the readiness, if necessary, to die." Martin van Creveld, *Fighting Power: German and American Military Performance, 1939-1945,* Westport, CT: Greenwood Press, 1982, p. 3.

25. Tucker, *op. cit.,* p. 64.

26. See Record, *op. cit.,* pp. 36-37; John E. Mueller, "The Search for the 'Breaking Point' in Vietnam: The Statistics of a Deadly Quarrel," *International Studies Quarterly,* December 1980, pp. 507-511.

27. Record, *op. cit.,* p. 37.

28. Richard K. Betts, "Interests, Burdens, and Persistence: Asymmetries Between Washington and Hanoi," *International Studies Quarterly,* December 1980, p. 523.

29. Anthony Shadid and Sewell Chan, "Protests Unleashed by Cleric Mark a New Front in War," *Washington Post,* April 5, 2004; Karl Vick and Saad Sarhan, "Eight U.S. Troops Killed in Shi'ite Uprising," *Washington Post,* April 5, 2004; Jeffrey Gettleman, "A Young Radical's Anti-US Wrath is Unleashed," *New York Times,* April 5, 2004; Rod Nordland, Melinda Liu, and Scott Johnson, "The Dark Road Ahead," *Newsweek,* April 12, 2004, *http://ebird.afis.osd.mil/ebfiles/20040405272720.html.*

30. Dana Priest, "The CIA's Anonymous Number 2," *Washington Post,* January 9, 2004.

31. Yochi J. Dreazen, "Iraq Bombings Underscore Security Challenge," *Wall Street Journal,* February 12, 2004.

32. Jim Krane, "U.S. Has Murky Picture of Iraqi Resistance," Associated Press on line, February 15, 2004; "Insurgents Threaten to Take Over Cities When Troops Leave," *USA Today,* February 5, 2004.

33. "Battling for Iraq's Future," *Middle East International,* January 9, 2004, p. 4; Danna Harman, "Baathists Need Not Apply," *Christian Science Monitor,* May 28, 2003.

34. Joshua Hammer, "Holding the Line," *Newsweek,* February 16, 2004, p. 33; Jackie Calmes, "Foreign Fighters in Iraq Are Few But Lethal," *Wall Street Journal,* February 12, 2004.

35. Jim Muir, "'Al Qaeda' Influence Grows in Iraq," BBC News, July 24, 2003.

36. "U.S. Warns of More Iraqi Attacks," BBC News, August 10, 2003.

37. Edward Wong, "Up to 80 Killed at Bomb Blast at 2 Iraqi Sites," *New York Times*, February 11, 2004.

38. Coauthor (W. Andrew Terrill) interviews with U.S. Army officers returning from Iraq.

39. Record, *op. cit.*, pp. 81-82.

40. Douglas S. Blaufarb, *The Counterinsurgency Era: U.S. Doctrine and Performance, 1950 to the Present*, New York: Free Press, 1977, p. 252.

41. Clodfelter, *op. cit.*, p. 776.

42. H.R. McMaster, *Dereliction of Duty: Lyndon Johnson, Robert McNamara, the Joint Chiefs of Staff, and the Lies That Led to Vietnam*, New York: HarperCollins, 1997, pp. 143-144.

43. See Jeffrey Record, "How America's Own Military Performance in Vietnam Aided and Abetted the 'North's' Victory"; Marc Jason Gilbert, ed., *Why the North Won the Vietnam War*, New York: Palgrave, 2003, pp. 121-123.

44. William W. Momyer, *Air Power in Three Wars*, Washington, DC: Office of History, U.S. Air Force, 1978, p. 95.

45. Henry Kissinger, *The White House Years*, Boston: Little, Brown, and Company, 1979, p. 1112.

46. David Hackworth and Julie Sherman, *About Face, The Odyssey of an American Warrior*, New York: Simon and Schuster, 1989, p. 534.

47. Ronald H. Spector, *After Tet: The Bloodiest Year of the War*, New York: Free Press, 1993, p. 79.

48. Shelby Stanton, *The Rise and Fall of an American Army: U.S. Ground Forces in Vietnam, 1965-1973*, Novato, CA: Presidio Press, 1985, p. 23; Ronald H. Spector, *op. cit.*, p. 43; James R. Ebert, *A Life in a Year: The American Infantryman in Vietnam, 1965-1972*, Novato, CA: Presidio Press, 1993, p. 1; Thomas C. Thayer, *War Without Fronts: The American Experience in Vietnam*, Boulder, CO: Westview Press, 1985, p. 94.

49. Bruce Palmer, Jr., *The 25-Year War: America's Military Role in Vietnam*, Lexington, KY: University Press of Kentucky, 1984, p. 69.

50. Deputy Secretary Paul D. Wolfowitz, in a March 11, 2003, speech to the Veterans of Foreign Wars, declared: "The people of Iraq understand what this crisis is about . . . Like the people of France in the 1940s, they view us as their hoped-for liberator." Less than a week later, Vice President Richard Cheney told NBC's *Meet the Press*: "I think things have gotten so bad inside Iraq, from the standpoint of the American people, my belief is we will, in fact, be greeted as liberators." Both quoted in Susan Page, "Prewar Predictions Coming Back to Bite," *USA Today*, April 1, 2003. After the war, Wolfowitz conceded that "It was difficult to imagine before the war that the criminal gang of sadists and gangsters who have run Iraq for 35 years would continue fighting . . . what has been sometimes called a guerrilla war." Quoted in Matt Kelley, "Pentagon's Wolfowitz Admits U.S. Erred in Iraq," Associated Press, July 24, 2003.

51. Daniel Williams, "U.S. Team Hunts Lethal Low-Tech Insurgency," *Washington Post*, February 5, 2004.

52. Alissa J. Rubin, "Strikes at 'Collaborators' Sow Fear But Not Flight," *Los Angeles Times*, February 12, 2004.

53. Blaufarb, *op. cit.*, pp. 221-242.

54. Richard A. Hunt, *Pacification: The American Struggle for Vietnam's Hearts and Minds*, Boulder, CO: Westview Press, 1995, p. 204.

55. Tucker, *op. cit.*, p. 315.

56. Blaufarb, *op. cit.*, p. 263; Hunt, *op. cit.*, pp. 253-255.

57. *Ibid.*, pp. 266-267; Tucker, *op. cit.*, p. 219.

58. Hunt, *op. cit.*, pp. 247-251; Blaufarb, *op. cit.*, pp. 270-271.

59. Hunt., *op. cit.*, pp. 217-220.

60. *Ibid.*, pp. 267-268.

61. Jeff Wilkenson, "U.S. Raids 'A Work in Progress'," *Miami Herald*, November 24, 2003.

62. "U.S. Forces Pound Iraqi Insurgents," BBC News Online, November 18, 2003.

63. Barbara Plett, "Fighting for Hearts of Iraq Sunnis," BBC News, March 16, 2004. Internet.

64. Stanton, *op. cit.*, p. 333; Tucker, *op. cit.*, pp. 214-215.

65. Stanley Robert Larsen and James Lawton Collins, Jr., *Allied Participation in Vietnam,* Washington, DC: Department of the Army, 1975, pp. 124-145.

66. Tucker, *op. cit.*, pp. 459-460.

67. *Ibid.*, pp. 458-459, 462-463.

68. Anderson, *op. cit.*, p. 290.

69. Douglas Pike, *Vietnam and the Soviet Union: Anatomy of an Alliance,* Boulder, CO: Westview Press, 1987, 1987, pp. 199-123. Also see Ilya V. Gaiduk, *The Soviet Union and the Vietnam War*, Chicago: Ivan R. Dee, 1996, pp. 58-64.

70. Chen Jian, "China's Involvement in the Vietnam War, 1964-1969," *The China Quarterly,* June 1995, pp. 378-380. During 1964-69, a total of 320,000 Chinese troops served in North Vietnam; the deployment peaked in 1967 at 170,000. Also see Qiang Zhai, *China and the Vietnam Wars, 1950-1975,* Chapel Hill, NC: University of North Carolina Press, 2000.

71. Cordesman, *op. cit.*, pp. 37-40.

72. Paul Richter, "Bush Urges Resolve on Iraq," *Los Angeles Times*, March 17, 2004.

73. Numbers are current as of November 2003. See "Foreign Forces in Iraq," *Middle East International*, November 21, 2003, p. 8; Vernon Loeb, "20,000 Allied Troops to Aid U.S. Effort to Stabilize Iraq," *Washington Post*, June 19, 2003.

74. *Ibid.*, and "Poland Pledges to Keep Troops in Iraq," *London Financial Times*, March 17, 2004.

75. "Australia May Keep Troops in Sovereign Iraq," *Jordan Times*, March 24, 2004.

76. Freddy Cuevas, "Troops from Honduras to Leave Iraq on Time," *Miami Herald*, March 17, 2004.

77. See Arirang TV Report, "Launching Ceremony of Korean Troops to be Dispatched to Iraq Will Be Held on February 23," as cited by Foreign Broadcast Information Service (hereafter FBIS), February 15, 2004; Ryu Jin, "Korean Troops to Head for Iraq April 7," *Korean Times*, March 9, 2004; "U.S. Allies Reconsider Iraq Mission," BBC News Online, March 19, 2004.

78. "Kyodo: Japan, Britain Agree on Greater UN Iraq Involvement," Tokyo Kyodo World Service, February 13, 2004, as cited by FBIS, February 13, 2004; "Sending Japan Troops to Iraq Historic Mistake," *Jordan Times*, February 13, 204; David Polling, "Death of Japanese Troops in Iraq 'Would Spur Reform'," *London Financial Times*, March 3, 2004.

79. David R. Sands, "U.S. Allies Pressured to Justify War Support," *Washington Times*, February 17, 2004.

80. See Ang Cheng Guan, *Ending the Vietnam War: The Vietnamese Communists' Perspective,* New York: RoutledgeCurzon, 2004, pp. 150-165; Van Tien Dung, *Our Great Spring Victory: An Account of the Liberation of South Vietnam,* John Spragens, Jr., trans., New York: Monthly Review Press, 1977, pp. 6-25.

81. The departure of U.S. combat forces left about 550,000 South Vietnamese regulars and 525,000 territorials to face a PAVN estimated at 500,000-600,000 troops, about 220,000 of which were in South Vietnam. Jeffrey J. Clarke, *Advice and Support: The Final Years, The U.S. Army in Vietnam,* Washington, DC: Center of Military History, U.S. Army, 1988, p. 495.

82. See Record, *op. cit.*, pp. 122-140.

83. Joseph Buttinger, *Vietnam: The Unforgettable Tragedy,* New York: Horizon Press, 1977, p. 148.

84. Vao Van Vien, *The Final Collapse,* Washington, DC: U.S. Army Center of Military History, 1983, p. 155.

85. See, for example, Evan Thomas, *The Very Best Men--Four Who Dared: The Early Years of the CIA,* New York: Simon and Schuster, 1995, p. 328.

86. *The Pentagon Papers: The Defense Department History of United States Decisionmaking on Vietnam,* Vol. 4, Boston: Beacon Press, 1971, pp. 398-399.

87. Douglas Kinnard, *The War Managers: American Generals Reflect on Vietnam,* New York: Da Capo Press, 1977, p. 97.

88. Stephen T. Hosmer, Konrad Kellen, and Brian M. Jenkins, *The Fall of South Vietnam: Statements by Vietnamese Military and Civilian Leaders,* Santa Monica, CA: Rand Corporation, 1978, p. 31.

89. Stuart A. Herrington, *Peace With Honor? An American Reports on Vietnam, 1973-1975,* Novato, CA: Presidio Press, 1983, p. 40.

90. See Clarke, *op. cit.*, pp. 341-359.

91. Anthony James Joes, *The War for South Vietnam, 1954-1975*, Rev. Ed., Westport, CT: Praeger, 2001, pp. 150-151.

92. Eric M. Bergerud, *The Dynamics of Defeat: The War in Hau Nghia Province*, Boulder, CO; Westview Press, 1991, p. 81.

93. See Clarke, *op. cit.*, pp. 42-42, 112, 114-116, 216, 314, 331, 345-346, 348, 363, 385-388, 408.

94. Guenter Lewy, *America in Vietnam*, New York: Oxford University Press, 1978, p. 218.

95. William J. Duiker, *The Communist Road to Power in Vietnam*. Second ed., Boulder, CO; Westview Press, 1996, pp. 350, 359.

96. Timothy J. Lomperis, *The War Everyone Lost--and Won: America's Intervention in Viet Nam's Twin Struggles*, Rev. Ed., Washington, DC: Congressional Quarterly Press, 1993, p. 160.

97. *Ibid.*, p. 160.

98. Henry A. Kissinger, "The Vietnam Negotiations," *Foreign Affairs*, Vol. 47, 1969, p. 230.

99. George C. Herring, *America's Longest War: The United States and Vietnam, 1950-1975*, Third ed., New York: McGraw-Hill, 1996, p. 298.

100. See Jeffrey Record, *Dark Victory, America's Second War with Iraq*, Annapolis, MD: Naval Institute Press, 2003, pp. 87-91.

101. "Text: Iraqi Interim Constitution," BBC News, March 8, 2004, internet.

102. Dexter Filkins, "Iraqis Receive U.S. Approval of Constitution," *New York Times*, March 2, 2004.

103. Quoted in Matthew Clark, "Sistani Says Iraq Constitution a 'Dead End'," *Christian Science Monitor*, March 23, 2004.

104. Anthony Shadid and Colum Lynch, "Shi'ite Cleric Threatens to Shun U.N. Envoys in Iraq," *Washington Post*, March 23, 2004.

105. Michael M. Gunter, "The Kurdish Question in Perspective, *World Affairs*, Vol. 166, No. 4, Spring 2004, pp. 201-204.

106. Barbara Plett, ""Fighting for Hearts of Iraqi Sunnis," BBC News, March 16, 2004, internet.

107. See Andreas Wimmer, "Democracy and Ethno-Religious Conflict in Iraq," *Survival,* Winter 2003-04, pp. 11-134.

108. Quoted in Reuters, December 6, 2003.

109. International Crisis Group, *Iraq: Building a New Security Structure,* Baghdad/Brussels, IGC Middle East Report No. 20, December 2003, pp. 1-22; T. Christian Miler, "Coalition to Reopen Bidding for Iraqi Military Contract, *Los Angeles Times,* February 28, 2004, internet.

110. Cordesman, *op. cit.,* 554. Also see Record, *Dark Victory, op. cit.,* pp. 141-142.

111. International Crisis Group, "Iraq: Building a New Security Structure," *ICG Middle East Report,* No. 20, p. 15.

112. Rajiv Chandrasekaran, "U.S. to Form New Iraqi Army," *Washington Post,* April 13, 2003; Patrick E. Tyler, "U.S.-British Project: To Build a Postwar Iraqi Armed Force of 40,000 Soldiers in Three Years," *New York Times,* June 24, 3003.

113. "U.S. to Begin Recruiting for New Army," *Washington Post,* November 5, 2003.

114. Christine Spolar, "Iraqi Soldiers Deserting New Army," *Chicago Tribune,* December 9, 2003.

115. Rowan Scarborough, "Colonel in Iraq Refuses to Resign," *Washington Times,* October 31, 2003.

116. Associated Press, "U.S. Military Expects Attacks on Iraqi Policemen to Escalate," *Baltimore Sun,* March 26, 2004.

117. Rod Nordland, Melinda Liu, and Scott Johnson, "The Dark Road Ahead," *Newsweek,* April 12, 2004, p. 30.

118. Christine Hauser, "Ready or Not Help from New Iraqi Forces is Vital U.S. Military Says," *New York Times,* April 12, 2004, internet.

119. Major General Martin Dempsey, "Coalition Provisional Authority Briefing on Ongoing Operations of Task Force 1st Armored Division and Iraqi Civil Defense Corps in Baghdad," U.S. Department of Defense News Transcript, February 2, 2004, internet.

120. Theola Labbe, "Iraq's New Military Taking Shape," *Washington Post,* September 16, 2003; Bradley Graham, "Touring Iraq, Rumsfeld Gets Upbeat Assessment," *Washington Post,* December 7, 2003; "Rumsfeld Lauds Performance

of Iraqi Security Forces," U.S. Department of State Bureau of International Information Programs, October 21, 2003, internet.

121. Greg Jaffe, "Iraqis Struggle with Tough Job: Fighting Insurgents," *Wall Street Journal*, February 24, 2004.

122. Michael R. Gordon, "Iraq Insurgency Spreads, U.S. Finds More Foes and Fewer Friends," *New York Times*, April 9, 2004, internet.

123. See W. Andrew Terrill, *Nationalism Sectarianism, and the Future of Post-Saddam Iraq*, Carlisle, PA: Strategic Studies Institute, U.S. Army War College, July 2003.

124. Dean Rusk, with Richard Rusk and Daniel S. Papp, *As I Saw It*, New York: W. W. Norton, 1990, p. 497.

125. Stanley Karnow, "Giap Remembers," *New York Times Magazine*, June 23, 1990, p. 36.

126. See Record, *op. cit.*, pp. 54-56; Joes, *op. cit.*, pp. 101-104; Duiker, *op. cit.*, pp. 295-297; Lomperis, *op. cit.*, pp. 76-80; Gabriel Kolko, *Anatomy of a War: Vietnam, the United States, and the Modern Historical Experience*, New York: W. W. Norton, 1985, pp. 334-337.

127. See John E. Mueller, *War, Presidents and Public Opinion*, New York: John Wiley and Sons, 1973, pp. 52-58; Eric V. Larson, *Casualties and Consensus: The Historical Role of Casualties in Domestic Support for U.S. Military Operations*, Santa Monica, CA; Rand Corporation, 1996, pp. 59-66.

128. Larson, *op. cit.*, pp. 27-29.

129. See Mueller, *op. cit.*; Larson, *op. cit.*; Lorell and Kelley, *op. cit.*, and Benjamin C. Schwarz, *Casualties, Public Opinion, and U.S. Military Intervention: Implications for U.S. Regional Strategies*, Santa Monica, CA: Rand Corporation, 1994. Also see discussion in Peter D. Feaver and Christopher Gelpi, *Choosing Your Battles: American Civil-Military Relations and the Use of Force*, Princeton, NJ: Princeton University Press, 2003, pp. 95-148; Richard A. Lacquement, Jr., "The Casualty Aversion Myth," *Naval War College Review*, Winter 2004, pp. 38-57; John A. Gentry, "Military Force in an Age of National Cowardice," *Washington Quarterly*, Autumn 1998, pp. 179-191; Jeffrey Record, "Force Protection Fetishism: Sources, Consequences, and (?) Solutions," *Aerospace Power Journal*, Summer 2000, pp. 4-11.

130. See Peter Feaver and Christopher Gelpi, "Casualty Aversion: How Many Deaths Are Acceptable? A Surprising Answer," *Washington Post*, November 7, 1999.

131. Larson, *op. cit.*, p. 15.

132. Richard K. Betts, "What Will It Take to Deter the United States?" *Parameters,* Winter 1995-96, p. 76.

133. Jeffrey Kimball, *Nixon's Vietnam War,* Lawrence, KS: University Press of Kansas, 1998, pp. 72-74.

134. Anderson, *op. cit.*, pp. 286, 290.

135. CNN.com, "Special Report, War in Iraq: U.S. and Coalition Casualties," Internet.

136. Lorrell and Kelley, *op. cit.*, p. 6.

137. Quoted in *Ibid.*, p. 80.

138. See Mueller, *op. cit.*, Jeffrey S. Milstein, *Dynamics of the Vietnam War: A Quantitative Analysis and Predictive Computer Simulation,* Columbus, OH: Ohio State University Press, 1974; Samuel Kernell, "Explaining Presidential Popularity; How Ad Hoc Theorizing, Misplaced Emphasis, and Insufficient Care in Measuring One's Variables Refuted Common Sense and Led Conventional Wisdom Down the Path of Anomalies," *American Political Science Review,* June 1978, pp. 503-519.

139. For a recent exposition of this view by a prominent historian and neoconservative commentator, see Victor Davis Hanson, "The Utility of War," *Quarterly Journal of Military History,* Winter 2003, pp. 1-15. Also See Russell Weigley, *The American Way of War, op. cit.*

140. See Record, *Dark Victory, op. cit.*, pp. 199-123; Purdum, *op. cit.*, pp. 231-233.

141. Frank Newport, "Approval for Handling of War in Iraq Jumps, Little Change in Basic Support for U.S. Involvement in War," *The Gallup Poll Tuesday Briefing,* December 19, 2003, pp. 25-27.

142. "American Public Opinion About the Situation in Iraq," February 3, 2004, *http://www.gallup.com/poll/focus/sr030610.asp.*

143. Richard Morin and Dana Milbank, "Support for Bush Falls on Economy and Iraq," *Washington Post,* March 9, 2004; John Harwood, "Economic Fears May Threaten Bush's Job," *Wall Street Journal,* March 11, 2004.

144. "American Public Opinion About Iraq," The Gallup Organization, April 13, 2004, *http://www.gallup.com/pool/focus/sr030610.asp.*

145. See Jeffrey Record, *Making War, Thinking History: Munich, Vietnam, and Presidential Uses of from Korea to Kosovo,* Annapolis, MD: Naval Institute Press, 2002.

146. See Anthony Cordesman, "The Facts We Must Face," *Washington Post,* April 4, 2004.

147. Richard Nixon, *No More Vietnams,* New York: Avon Books, 1985, p. 88.

148. See David Ignatius, "What Iran Wants in Iraq," *Washington Post,* February 27, 2004.

149. *Ibid.*

CPSIA information can be obtained
at www.ICGtesting.com
Printed in the USA
LVHW091216280820
664428LV00001B/173